The Loony's Royalties

Iza Chkadua

Translated by Ekaterine Machitidze

authorHOUSE®

AuthorHouse™ UK Ltd.
500 Avebury Boulevard
Central Milton Keynes, MK9 2BE
www.authorhouse.co.uk
Phone: 08001974150

First published by AuthorHouse   05/10/2011

ISBN: 978-1-4567-7706-7 (sc)
ISBN: 978-1-4567-7707-4 (e)

Contents

The one-way ticket

He was sitting just by my side, I knew for sure. I could not realize then whether it was him or just his double. It appeared when Luka (it was his name) showed the blue glasses that I had given as a keepsake and sang my favorite solo in a low voice. I was gripped by fear. The appearance was as clear and obvious as the letters that I can see on the white desktop of my computer now. It made me remember the man who was dead. I had witnessed his burial. Though, he was there again. In what we call reality he led a life of an ordinary man. He had eyes deep blue and striking and the straw-colored hair fell down from the forehead right into them. Sometimes he looked through a place to another as if he was going to make a slow movie shot or just move at a slow speed. I had never seen anyone with such a wonderful gaze and with a temper so very quiet. It was his character to think much and talk less. When he deceased we all mourned and cried. A year later he started to appear now here, now there and the appearance had nothing in common with the desires and thoughts. It was not a shade, it was really him.

I thought much how to make you interested in the story and how to prove that it happened in truth. Please don't blame me for being insincere. Though , the only way to alley the suspicions is to tell the story from the very beginning.

I was a student and I used to go out early in the morning as all students do. It took just five minutes to walk from the bus station to the Institute. I always followed the road silently and always felt someone pacing by my side. I had never looked in the direction to see who it was. I had no doubts. You know, we all stride somewhere in a hurry in the morning and there is nothing strange about that.

I was waiting for the bus that happened to be too late. There were much people crowded at the stop. I was nervous a bit for I did not want to miss the lecture on Georgian Literature. Suddenly a wine red taxi stopped. The boy who stepped along the street abreast with me just a few minutes ago, was looking at me from the glass of the car now.

"I will take you to the Institute, it's on my way," – he said lovingly, though with respect. I was to run away for fear. I knew he was dead and wanted to go far away from the car, but I got into the taxi instead. I could not understand what had made me sit there then. When we started to come up the Vake Slope I realized that we were together. He stopped the taxi at the institute and pointed me to get off smilingly. I was as gentle and dutiful as a kid behaving blamelessly for he is waiting for the promised ice-cream.

The dream was continued during the lecture. I went to the ladies to get rid of the nightmare and splashed some water right into my face. On my way back I ran into a boy who had just tore himself away from the toilet. –"You saw him"?- he asked and the threatened expression of his face was a hint for me to guess who he was talking about. I turned back instinctively. I knew that he should be there. I was right. Sitting on the lime-tree branch he was looking into my face through the toilet window on the second floor.

It is not hard to catch up the sensations that people usually experience in the moments like that. I asked my group-mate to see me home for I had a headache and could not go home alone. We both went out.

Nina took my arm and then made a sudden movement. She opened her bag as if she had forgotten something and gave me a painkiller. Willing to free myself from the nightmare I swallowed another pill without water and we got on a bus.

Somebody let me have his seat for it was obvious that I felt unwell. When I turned to thank the man I saw those wonderful and sad deep blue eyes again. He was holding out two tickets. Though I took them, I don't remember how it happened. I was looking at the scrap of paper in my hand trying to sense whether it was real or not. When the bus stopped again he got off and crossed the street.

–"Who was that"?-asked Nina looking in a wide-eyed astonishment. I kept silent for I failed to find a right response. "He liked you", -she kept talking. I decided to go and see the grave at any price. I knew for sure that it was not a double. It was my Luka. And I thought somebody had dug him out of the tomb.

We used to sing in a company together. We knew that we had fallen in love with each other, but we preferred not to talk about the feeling. "What a sweet voice you have, Nekah"!-he told me and turned red in the face. "Your eyes are the most wonderful ones", - I answered and blushed. When one of the concerts was over I gave him some spectacles with blue glasses. They stressed the color of his eyes. I bought the glasses in Paris for him. "Take and keep the eyes hidden for me"!-I said. He took my palm in one hand while carrying the specs in another and uttered some brief phrases of love. I did not get a wink of sleep that night. I could not afford the time to sleep. I just wanted to think about him again and again reveling each minute of the thinking of the type. Yes, I was crazy about him.

I took some flowers to the cemetery where nothing had changed but the grass that was waving on the grave. The expression of his face on the marble was as gloomy as usual. I don't know how I dared to go there alone then. I sat downs on a stone and started to brood over him. A sudden fear struck me. It has already started to grow dark. I could not make my shivering body stand up and go. He watched me sitting on the metal railing just on the opposite side. I ran down the slope as fast as I could and cried out: "Go, leave me alone, go"! An old man opened the door of his car. When I set down he asked who the person who had gone was. The man took me home.

He came in my dream that night. He wondered what had made me so much afraid. The warm tone of his words forced me forward. "You are dead. How it happens that you are here now"?-I asked. "It's my soul",-he answered and disappeared not willing to be given any more questions again.

It was in summer. I had gone to the seaside with some friends of mine. The lanterns lit the night bar in Batumi. We were young and happy. I wanted to have a walk along the coast alone.

Looking at the water sparkling in blue gleams I dreamt of love as warm and tender as I had already experienced with him. Somebody passed by my side and just in a jiffy he was there. He was sad, calm and loving. Standing abreast with him I tried to compare the color of his eyes and the blue of the water. They both had eyes of the same color, though his ones were gloomy.

When I turned to the girls who had come nearer with their ice-creams he disappeared like soap bubble do. "Who was the guy"? - asked Lizi. "Nobody has been here", - I sad and she got that it was a secret. I was upset because of the words for I did not want him to be angry with me. I was even afraid for Luka was always there and always knew what was going on.

He used to come to me from time to time. I could see him sitting in a café or in transport beside me. Then he disappeared for a period of time that was quite long. I even started to forget him. In the autumn a heavy storm broke in the windows. A fir-tree dug out with its roots fell down on somebody's car in the yard. Mom asked me to take the linen from the clothe-line and started to close the windows. On the balcony somebody grasped my hand. It was him trying to drag me into the room. A few minutes later a sudden noise made us know that the balcony and a part of the loggia had already crashed down.

I got acquainted with a boy who turned out to be much attentive and considerate to me. He used to wait for me at the house every single day, sent me flowers and we went for a ride together. In winter he brought me some enormous roses and repeated convincingly that I was going to be his spouse. I took the words for kidding, though it is not a usual thing when a man even having fallen in love makes thing like those he did.

We got married. The wedding party was magnificent. I hardly managed to see the other end of the huge table so pompously set. I was going up the stairs dressed in that white dress and tiny white flowers plaited in the hair when I saw him. His calmness had disappeared. The taciturn guy talked too much. I heard none of his words for the happiness had made me perplexed. According to his face one might have thought that the words were the ones of congratulation. My fiancé asked me who was the boy standing by my side. It was not easy to tell the truth about the dead man and I answered that it was just an old acquaintance of mine. The same fear came to me again. I knew that he heard the words that would necessarily make him feel pity.

In the morning the sun was shining right into my eyes. It was a sign for me: get up and start the new life! My husband had brought some tremendous roses and put them at the bed. I felt the smell of the flowers and realized that Luka would never come to me again for the time designated for being in touch with me was over last night. I was happy and that was all he needed so badly.

The freedom and its shades

They all had different tempers. The head of the family was a strict despot adhering to the principles of his own. His wife Nina was a woman reserved as a slave gratifying all the lusts of her husband. Their daughter was an only child so very silent and unpretentious in her childhood and so very self-defending now. She got married and two years later came back home. It happened to be quite arduous for her to be a wife of a jester. She was twenty years old when she unexpectedly took her parents unawares with a kiddy in her arms.

What's up? - frowned the man.

Cannot stand, dad, cannot stand...- and Keti burst out crying.

Well, you can stay here but I have to be in the know of each step. Never dare go out without my permission! Clear?! – There was somewhat of a menace but sympathy between the words.

Keti tried to explain but the attempt made her father even more exacting. She went into her room and wept out. Mom tried to enter her room and talk with the girl but the man shouted at his wife:

Don't dare come in... Come here! - And Nina turned round without any manifestation of resentment.

Yes, Vano was a head of the family governing all the things around him. Sure, he was the one who had to manage what we call a man's business but it was really needless what he did with respect to the women. The wife and the daughter had their own wishes, lives and desires, he knew. But what could he do with the disposition?! Everything that had been going on inside and outside the family had to be agreed with him. And if any of the women tried to act contrary to his rules he administered justice and mete out punishment in a manner, say, brutal.

Unfortunately he could not go out. He had some problems with his legs and had not left the eighth floor for eight years. Yes, if he could have a chance to go out...It would have been a relief for him and his family. He would have spent the surge of energy and get back to his wife and daughter having been already calmed down. The fact that he had no children but Keti was a tragedy of his. He was anxious to have four and more heirs. As for Keti, she considered it was even better that she had neither a sister nor a brother. They would have had to suffer like me with the despot, - thought the girl.

Keti took it hard that her father was so cruel and inflexible. She was too innocent. She would never hurt somebody's feelings but it anyone tried to wrong her she immediately started to defend herself. And the type of self-defense was a thing that she permanently needed with her father – the dictator.

Once a boy who was in the same year as she called Keti. And the man set up a clamor again. When the man insisting on getting an explanation met the self-defense, he gave his daughter a slap in the face...

How dare you, you, even argue?! – the same was the thing with her mother always blaming the girl:

Don't' argue, dear! He's your father.

The never-ending support offered by the woman to her husband drove Keti to despair. All in tears she used to run to her friends just to cry on somebody's shoulder over there. She ran down the stairs of the eighth floor just like a small girl. She was forty and because of the slim constitution looked like one twenty-five years old.

Quite often room she wept roughly sitting in her: - why does he have such a character... What's so wrong with me, - she worried for she loved the man and was always searching for his warmth.

When the grand-daughter grew up it was her character that came into the picture. Too willful and naughty she had nothing in common with her mom. She could hardly get on with anyone in the family, neither with her mother nor with the grandparents. They failed to understand her too. She protested against the strictest grandpa. The grandmother was a dummy for her for the woman was too patient. As for her mother, they always had an argument against each other. She was so rude that it was impossible for her to find someone to get in love with. Later she softened and shouted at her mother even rarely. Sometimes, when she was in a good mood she managed to agree with her mom.

They were all cramped in the apartment with just two rooms. The old couple slept in the bed-room. Keti and her daughter slept in the living room. Even getting old did not make Vano change his attitudes. The eighty-five-years-old man held his own and still relied upon his fisticuffs when dealing with the problems of the family. He got more furious against everyone who had an opposite view and did not swear blind obedience to him.

At night the wife and husband locked in the room and used to talk till the morning. The woman had some problems with the ear. She was almost deaf. She bought a hearing aid but had not used it yet.

It hot now, I'll put in on in winter. Hm, in winter...why in winter, she did not know.

No, I can't get used to it, and the kerchief...and she found nsome other reason. She always kept the apparatus by her bed, though she never put it on. On nights, when the sleep wouldn't have come to the old couple just wanting to talk, the woman made her husband cry at the top of his voice. He had to repeat each phrase three and four times. The shouting man woke up his daughter and the grand-child sleeping in the next room. And the two started to knock against the wall then.

- Let us sleep, oh, let us sleep, - and the pairs from the two sides of the wall, so very angry with each other were awake throughout the nights.

There was a TV set in the living room. In the daytime, when Keti and her daughter were at work, the old people used to watch TV. They watched everything from politics to serials. It did no matter for them what a program was about. They were always interested in it. Watching TV had turned into something most important in their life. Because of Nina's problems with hearing her husband consoled her with a special gaze that he'd tell her everything at night. A frame passed after another for Nina watching all the programs in an inert way. Then it was a turn of the next generation - mom and her daughter who sat over there after the eleventh hour till 02:00 AM. And the schedule worked in the family like the supremacy of law.

Tamar was to finish school and had been getting ready for an excursion. She was going to take Keti with her. The news made Vano to bawl in such a manner that the neighbors just burst into his flat.

- Don't dare cross the threshold, – shouted the man all the evening, - take care not to do that! Whom do you take yourself for…I'll show you…notwithstanding the position of her grandpa, in the morning Tamar went for an excursion, though Keti failed to be courageous enough to follow her. She stayed at home and was too disappointed.

Once she met a man from America at her friend's place. He liked her. Keti was pleased that Alex was so smiling and warm. It was the warmth of a man that she had been lacking since the time. She agreed to have a date with a bachelor physicist who turned out to be a very pleasant person. Every single day he asked her to marry him. Keti having a grudge against her family decided to get married and in three months left for America with the man. Her father swore first fisting against the table finally he somehow got accustomed to the fact and finally plunged in a tired silence.

Just in a few months his granddaughter got married too. Though it was Vano's grandchild who had made the step, Nina took the two marriages for something, say, usual.

- It's their decision and I have no right to meddle in; it's not my business, - thought the woman and kept silent. Having already used to the position of a slave she thought she had no right to express her own opinion. She wished them joy…Though, the grandfather swore and fisted again. Then he took some heart drops and ultimately calmed down.

The old couple was left alone. They both suffered from an unexpected sorrow. It was Vano who could not stand the hush caused by their walkout. There was no one to argue against and no reason to expend his energies. His wife is resigned to him as a serf and he is the one who is always in need of someone to be against. He missed the way that he had been holding over the family for years and the resistance of Keti and her daughter. It was not easy to lose the position all of a sudden. The complete obedience of his wife does not make him feel a sense of relief. It's opposition that he enjoys too much. A conflict - it's his battle and his victory.

And he started to implore his daughter to come back with her husband. He said he had some nest egg at the bank and wanted to buy a big house to live there in a harmony with his daughter, his grandchild and their husbands. Keti wondered at the gentle tone of her father's and the supplication. It was a surprise, it was pleasant but it was unbelievable. She did not believe in such a change of the obstinate man and had decided to be just silent. She did not refuse to come back, though she said absolutely nothing about the arrival.

Vano called her in America each day and each day he asked her to move to Tbilisi. It was too hard for him to live alone and the desire to dwell together was so strong that it could easily make die if the wishes wouldn't come true. His expression had turned into something pitiful. One might have easily thought that he was ready to lick almost everyone's boot.

Two years passed. Vano, now suffering from sclerosis, hang up the receiver and started to dial the number again. Nina grasped the hearing aid to listen to him. His mild tone and the begging was so unusual that the woman used to put the apparatus off thinking that there was something wrong with it.

Come to us, honey! - He had never addressed his daughter this way. - Please come...- Finally his voice started to tremble. The man with his thrilling lips used to grab the receiver in his hands as an only hope of his.

As Keti stepped onto the boarding ramp of the plane her premature labor started. She was immediately taken to the clinic. In half an hour she gave birth to a baby boy. Right at the same time in one of Tbilisi clinics a man died from a heart attack. It was Vano.

She was told about it at the maternity hospital. She cried bitterly. Despite all the things she loved the man. She looked at the child with her eyes filled with tears, took him into her arms and wished him the only thing:

Don't do the same, please!

Behind the Curtain

It was a perfect watching place for the girl sitting right behind the curtain. She could see almost everything, though the object under observation had no idea of what had been going on. But what a secret it is if no one can ever divulge the truth. She decided to watch the stranger that she had noticed in the balcony for some days.

There was nothing strange in the fact that someone could manage to catch sight of her as well. He smoked a cigarette each half an hour on the balcony. There was always a girl glaring in such an unusual manner in the fourth floor window. He had never seen her before. She seemed to have been staying with the hosts and looking through the window was a method for her to amuse herself or just to spend time. Soon after he caught the first glance of the observer his surprised staring made the girl even confused. She decided to hide herself behind the curtain. Soon she appeared again silently looking at the balcony of the second floor.

She was probably in the seventh or in the eighth form, so very tiny and fragile. He was about twenty-five.

The boy always looking towards the window of the fourth floor had already become very much attached to the girl. It was a victory and she was proud of it. Yes, he noticed her. To cut a long story short, no matter what time it was, they tried to see each other.

She even noticed that it were Marlboro cigarettes that the guy used to smoke. Always in jeans the boy wore T-shirts of different colors. Sometimes with a sports bag on his bag he went out. She decided that he was a boxer or maybe a fighter and worked at a gym.

Thinking of the boy she did not sleep a wink at night. She spent days being on watch of the boy coming out of the building. One fine day with his bag on the back he came out through the front door. She immediately opened the door and rushed down the stairs. The uncle met her on the first floor. "What a hurry"!-said the man, though the girl did not stop and ran down.

She did not answer the surprised yard keeper putting his broom on the back too. She crossed the road and started to observe both sides of the street. Where could he have gone?! She noticed someone looking just like the guy and ran after him so as the cars moving in two lines stopped.

He entered a shop. She ran up the stairs and decided to stand beside. He bought cigarettes. It was a box of the Kent tobacco and she breathed a sigh of relief. She could face him without any embarrassment. He had nothing in common with the young man. She turned away and left the shop with her face looking so very sad then.

She did not hear even the assistant asking whether she could help her or not. She buried her head into the shoulders and went home.

In the evening she saw the boy looking towards her again and he went out the house with his bag on the back the next day too. Though, the girl failed to see him in the street once again. She just could not run down from the fourth floor in time and he was quick enough to disappear meanwhile.

It was time for her to leave the hosts. Her father arrived in the city to take the girl back. She stood at the window of the bedroom for a long time but in vain. The man from the corridor asked her to hurry up quite many times. She could not make a step. She was so very eager to see him again before leaving but there was no one on the balcony. With a pain in her heart she decided to write some words on the damp window. She scribbled: "Good Bye, Themo"!

Two years passed and she thought about him again. There was no one to tell about the secret feeling. She used to be always gloomy. When she left school her father took her to the city again to take the entrance exams. She should live at her uncle's place and it was so very good to have the opportunity back to see him through the window, get acquainted with him and get close friends with the man she used to call Themo for some reason.

In the evening all of them watched TV. She excused herself as if she was going to busy herself with reading and went to the bedroom. She was overjoyed. The color of the curtain foresaw the moments of happiness. Just a simple movement and the long wished time should come back.

Standing right at the window with her heart beating with joy she realizes that the things take place in the reality. She is waiting for the boy she left two years ago without ceremony and any notice. Now she has come back to him and nothing shall ever make her leave him. She has turned into a grown woman able to get acquainted with him and talk with him. And there is nothing strange about it.

When the door of the balcony opened she saw a girl with brown hair coming out of the room and carrying a linen copper in her hands. She put the copper by her side and wee trousers, shirts and panties made a string along the cloth-line.

Trying to understand what is going on she could not believe her eyes. A few minutes later she noticed the same girl with chestnut-colored hair coming out of the front door. She ran up the stairs of the shop nearby and went out with a bag full of bread.

The troubled girl waiting for the guy to appear on the balcony even thought that he had moved from the flat and some other people had been living there.

Two days passed for the girl waiting for the guy. And viola, suddenly someone opened the door of the balcony, slowly looked back and brought a pram out. Then the same person brought a baby. Yes, yes, it was him. He had not changed at all. The blue jeans, the T-shirt of white color again. The man smiling and fondling the kid seemed to be happy.

She felt something like opacity. Streams of tears ran down the wet cheeks to the trembling chin. She grieved over the love and dreams that she had already lost. It was him who had made her to come to the city and decide to enter the institute of higher education. Everything that took place in her consciousness or in the real life had something in common with the man. What was she going to do now?

The girl driven torpid could not take her eyes from a single point. Suddenly it started to rain. It was a true cloud-burst. It was difficult for the vehicles to move along the street covered with water. The girl unexpectedly opened the window and cried out his name. When he heard someone calling him, Themo started. Involuntary a smile ran through his face as if he had met an old acquaintance of his or someone so very precious. Then he turned to the baby again. The girl seemed not to be surprised by the welcome of the type. The smile made her glad. She opened her hands wide as a lunatic. The boy had no time to say anything…Perhaps she wanted to see him better or maybe it was an unintentional movement, the girl jumped up on the windowswill, leaned forward and called "Themo" again. She lost equilibrium and fell down from the window.

"What happened, Themo"? –does not stop asking the girl with chestnut-colored hair. The boy stopped dead on the sidewalk cannon hear anything. The local inhabitants have gathered around him. The torrents of rain wash his wet body trembling all over from cold or pain. Grey spots of the rain water have embroidered his white T-shirt, and he is looking in the direction from where the girl fallen from the fourth floor has just been taken.

The rain covered the city. There was no one left in the street. The heavy, noisy rain falls down to the ground. In Chavchavadze Street corner, on the balcony wetted with the drops silently stands a boy called Themo. Full of sorrow and thoughtful he smokes a Marlboro with a shivering hand and looks towards the window of the fourth floor by stealth.

"Who was she, what was it and what happened? What made the girl so different from others"? – thinks Themo feeling himself a part of the horrible fact. Trying to understand how the girl managed to know his name he wondered what was her own one and why the feeling that one day entered the heart of an ordinary girl looking through the window had such a terrible ending.

My grandmas whip

(My granny told me the story when I was a nine-years-old girl suffering from temperature. She told me that I had to be as strong as she was…)

All the countrymen had already gone to the Sunday fair, but my granny. She did not hurry to go out. Manya, it was her name, cleaned up the house, walked around her majestic horse and petted it. When she had already got onto the saddle of the bridled animal in a smart manner so very unusual for the age, and was going to dart to the outskirts of the village the youngest boy asked the horsewoman to take him to the edge of the yard. The mother did not make her son wait. She leaned forward and took up the boy. Manya seated Gogi just in front of her and snapped a whip on the horse.

Everyone knew my Granny Manya in the neighborhood. In the mountainous region horses were considered to be the best vehicles to move from a place to another. Manya used to ride from a village to another on the horseback. Neither abysses nor the darkness could threaten her. The forty-years-old Svani woman had made her horse stop on the brink of a precipice more than once since the time when she was a girl. She was used to looking down into the depth of gulfs. Nobody took it for something special when she appeared straddling on her horse. People surrounded her. They loved her for her being courageous and fair.

She walked round the counters two times and did the shopping. She bought some food and presents for the children. When she was ready to go home, she looked at the horse with that examining gaze and suddenly caught a sight of Sergo telling her something from a distance quite long and looking right into her face with his artful eyes. It was a surprise. Manya could never stand the good-for-nothing man talking too much. When he got nearer he touched his moustache and asked her in a manner much characteristic of an idle talker:

How are you, darling? Have not you grown old, Manya? – he asked.

Manya found the tone of his words annoying and answered him in a loud voice:

-Go, go there! Out, out of my sight!

Sergo came to her even nearer and whispered right in the ear:

-Oh, how I loved you, remember? – (he was in a mood that makes it hard for people to stop flirting). The man smiling into her face touched the moustache proudly again. It dismayed her

11

to hear the last word. She felt insulted. With a fast movement of her hand she beat him on the back unmercifully. Again and again she scourged him so as Sergo turned out to be as kind as to cut a run. When crossing the bridge he could easily remind one a prisoner who has just escaped from the jail.

All the street vendors roared with laughter.

The crowd made fun of the man and blessed her, though Manya did not listen to them. She was beside with rage and her face expressed all the feelings that she experienced then. She hang all that she had bought on the saddle and went at full speed.

The darkness had already fallen when Manya left the horse in the stable and crossed the threshold of her house. Now the children surrounded her. They were just beside themselves with joy when they looked into the bag. Some of them had candy boxes, others put on their brand-new akhalukhis to put on under Cirkassian coats. Liza, the eldest among her children got a dress with a belt around the waist. They had never been as happy as they were then showing the clothes to each other with that hearty, free and easy laughter.

At night when, at about ten, some men rode their horses into their yard. She got up from the bed, slid apart the curtains and looked out stealthily. One of the five armed strangers was calling the head of the family. It was horror that she had to feel that moment for it was obvious that the men had come for something bad. They authoritatively insisted upon Jacob's coming out of the house.

Her husband had gained prestige with the countryside of the region. The well-read and soft-hearted man used to fight against injustice. He was accused of organizing a revolt. Yes, he had some complaints against the existing unfair authorities, though the charge had nothing in common with the reality.

He was too calm when the officials stormed into the room impudently. One of the new-comers told him to go before them and cuffed Jacob standing at the door. It was a great surprise for Jacob who would never let anyone to offend his dignity without response. Though, it was a different case now. There were his family behind him and Bosheviks in front of him who could treat almost everyone, women and children without mercy. He looked at them with that furious anger in his eyes and went downstairs shaking his head in a threatening manner.

The four kids wept out almost simultaneously. They looked at the road where their father walked in front of the five riding functionaries. Next morning three horsemen with some saddle-bags came to their place again. Manya had fallen ill and could not manage to get up from her bed.

We have to conduct a search of the house,-said one of them carrying a uniform on his arm and looked into the room impertinently. They searched all the drawers of the bureau and threw the bed clothes down on the floor. After having checked each corner of the rest of Jacob's house they decided to enter his bedroom. Grandma Manya who was ill in bed remembered that there was a gun hidden in Jacob's pillow. –"Don't come in"!-shouted the women to one of the officials of Cheka who had to step back. She had enough time to change the cushion and rested her head on the pillow with the gun.

-Don't listen to her, just go in!-said a bureaucrat to another mockingly and they dashed into the bedroom. Though, the officials failed to find any weapon there they turned the house upside-down and took the huge library into the yard. The fire made the kids cry and scream with fun.

Manya tried to calm the children down, though they took the enormous blaze for something wonderful and perfect and were not going to stop clapping their hands joyfully.

They made Jacob starve for seventeen days in the jail. They wanted him to name his accomplices but he was silent. The feeling of hunger was nothing as compared with the state of his mind so much disturbed by what they did.

Some days passed. He was extremely exhausted. One evening the sky darkened and a heavy rain began to fall down. A stream ran through the hole in the ceiling. Jacob was happy. He put his Svanetian hat off the head and when it was half filled with the water he took a sip of it. He drank four hats of water and when he finally slaked his thirst he fell asleep.

Next day the Bolsheviks let a knight-marshal of the post into his cell. He accused Jacob of organizing an uprising. The charged and the accuser were quite good acquaintances and Jacob could not understand what was it that could make a man to do such a shameful thing. He promised to take vengeance on the man for what he had done. The investigation failed to reveal any evidence against Jacob and they had to release him.

Manya equipped the horse again and went out of the house without uttering a syllable. She rode the galloping horse to the Sunday fair and hummed. One might have thought that she was going for something good and pleasant. In truth, she wanted to see Lado, the man who betrayed her husband. Jacob wanted to revenge himself upon Lado. The only way out of the feuds of the type in the region dealt with murder.

She leapt down from the horse and stepped into the depth of the fair. She saw Lado with a ten-litter vessel for wine in his hands laughing and telling something to the shop-keeper. Unexpectedly a whip lashed against his back made Lado stagger. A lash followed another until Sergo put his hand to his aching head and ran away. People gathered around her wondered what had made the woman so furious.

-It serves all the turncoats and avid ones right! - she said and left the place.

Jacob read a book at the fireplace. He raised his head from time to time and laughed in a loud voice. Tears ran down his eyes as if he was going to die laughing. It was her deed that made him to split his sides and forget that he was angry. Jacob asked Manya to tell him the story again and again and even felt some pity for Lado, the man beaten by a woman.

Yes, she did it! It was done! A man's revenge would have been much severe than her own one. She was happy and self-satisfied for she did her best to avoid the danger facing her family.

So what if I am dumb

He'd been dumb since he was born. He was so very handsome that people failed to take their eyes off him in the street. The lasses just stopped when they saw him. Though, he could not speak and always tried to keep off. He preferred not to get acquainted with them. He craved to have someone to be in love with but he had stifled all the desires to keep the muteness in secret. It was much better to be in the spotlight, to be the very one people were interested in than to experience the keen disappointment.

The unworried expression could easily make one think that he really had no problems. However, the reality differed and he took it hard to be in the situation. He had much changed since his mother died. He was always busy and always in a hurry. He used to walk with his shoulders straightened. His light step seemed to be so stately. He did everything with such a zeal. There was no book that he had not read yet. His mother had told their friends that he even wrote poetry in secret.

Yes, Data seemed to be almost untroubled, but he was too soft-hearted. When someone died in the neighborhood he always came to be there at once. He used to stand near at hand carrying a hanky with his long and delicate fingers and shed tears over the deceased. Thank God! Wedding parties were much frequent than all the funerals in the part of the city. The solemnities made him so happy that he could do nothing with the playful smile for it was impossible for him not to be glad when someone by his side was lucky or happy.

The mysterious wish for love was something just kept in his dreams and fantasies. They took it for haughtiness when he tried to look aside when all the girls stared at him. But in truth, he'd always been willing to be ugly and have the power of human speech.

One morning someone knocked at his door. When he opened the door he saw a stranger with a small girls standing beside. She was so fragile. The man had a large journal with a colored cover in his hand and the girl had a music book that served as a sign for him that the two were looking for the music teacher living over there. He pointed at the door and got back immediately to avoid any questions.

He often saw the girl who seemed to have been taking some private lessons there. Every other day he could hear the sounds of music wearing him out so much. And the sounds never changed.

He had a good ear for music, he loved music but the never-ending tapping over the keys got on his nerves. He used to dash to the window and bar it not to hear anything.

One day he got home and saw some strange words made with a red felt pen:

Music to hear, why hear'st thou music sadly?
Sweets with sweets war not, joy delights in joy.
W. Shakespeare

Data smiled. It was not difficult guess who had done it. He was pleased but he knew that she was too small and he was dumb. He started and tried not to pay attention to the thing. He took some rag from the room, though he failed to rub the lines out. Then he went down to the basement, brought a pot and a small brush from there and started to recolor the door with some white paint. When he got back he decided not to think about it for it was a childish prank and nothing more.

When he turned off the light and got ready to go to bed he remembered the brilliant sonnet by Shakespeare and the image of the tiny and delicate girl arose in his imagination. Then he remembered how he locked the windows and experienced the feeling of repentance. He could not sleep that night. "How strange she is...and how she managed to match the sonnet against my indifference", - he thought. Yes, he was sad.

Some days passed without remembering the girl. He had seen her neither walking up the stairs nor at the front door. Suddenly he felt a sudden feeling of melancholy. He was troubled somehow and looked out of the window one more time. Then he walked up and down the stairs and came to the calendar. It was Friday and she used to come to the teacher on Fridays. He stepped to the window quickly, opened it and tried to overhear. He sounds of the piano were coming again and he had a sigh of relief. The unexpectedness made him smile involuntarily. The music had stopped to unsettle him and he had stopped to experience the desire to escape from the sounds. Instead, he though the sounds were even pleasing.

Suddenly the sounds ceased and someone spurted against the window attracting his attention to the image of the girl looking through the glass. They smiled to each other all of a sudden. Then he waved his hand to her and told her something just moving his lips. She turned back immediately. He stood over there waiting for her and thinking that she was not small at all. - Maybe she's sixteen or seventeen... Maybe it makes no difference for her whether I can speak or no. He knew, he was such a good-looking young man.

He ran down the stairs hurriedly. Data seemed to be enraptured like a child. He made up his mind to wait for the girl and tell her that he was dumb who'd never be able to say anything to her. He was crumpling a scarf in his hand. It was cold and the wind taking the dry leaves from a place to another sounded like some sweet and blissful melody.

He did not notice her when she stopped by his side and said hello to him. He just nodded and hung his head. The welcome upset her. Looking right into his face she thought he did not like her. The girl who was to burst out crying put the bag on her shoulder and threw the music book into the ash can standing nearby. She turned back and ran away from the place. Data tried to cry something out but he managed to make some screaming sounds that made her stop and look back. She was dumbfounded and horrified. And she realized what had been going on and moved towards him with her arms outstretched and hugged him and said:

- You cannot speak, Data? – Mary touched his face with her fingers tenderly and looked into his eyes with sympathy.

He nodded. He seemed to be glad for she had called him by his name and she knew the truth about him... It seemed to be no problem for her...

- And what then? - went the girl on, - you are the best...

He could just move his head up and down. He was happy. - "And what then"?! - he'd never thought before.

He pointed with his hand to the ash can as if asking what was the problem with the music book. Mary got what he was about and said softly:

I don't care for music...I really don't...It was you who made me come here...I love you, you see?! Remember Vake Park?

Data tried to concentrate his attention. The ice cream café and the girls looking at him and talking with one another. A stranger and a dog that bit one of the girls then. "Dear my! Let me remember"! She raised her leg a bit and put her finger against the muscle with a scar on it. And he came to himself and made that odd scream once again. He took her in his arms, kissed her head against his heart and kissed her for joy.

He remembered the park, the ice cream café, the girls looking at him and talking with one another, the stranger and the dog that bit one of the girls then. Data was the first one who ran to the girl, took a snowy handkerchief from his pocket, dressed the wound tight and looked into the eyes of the threatened babe. Someone called in an ambulance... He had never seen her since the time.

However, she managed to find him. He was shaking out a cape covered with snow at the door when she walked down the stairs with an obvious feeling of satisfaction. He did not notice her then. He was shriveled up with cold and went in immediately. She ran out into the street and saw a sparrow sitting on a branch and said to it: -I've found him. Understand?!- It was not easy to hide the delight. She stood on her tiptoes telling the bird about the happiness. Then she shook the branch and put her face just against the snow falling down from it and rubbed it into the skin.

It was already daylight and he had not slept a wink yet. What had happened had too much in common with his dreams. He wanted to give a cry. He was happy. First he managed just to murmur some sounds, then he tried to utter some words and finally he shouted and shouted and shouted beginning to speak. He listened to the vowels and when he was sure his words were almost distinctly audible, he threw up the cut-glass vase standing on the table and cried to the photograph of his mother's hanging on the wall: "Mom, can you hear me...Can I speak, mom? You hear me"? Then he rushed out and knocked at the door of the music teacher. The woman darted out and made a gesture trying to make it out what was going on.

I love you Donara! Please play something! Play until Shakespeare is alive, until people sing and dance "Daisi[1]", until life is the most precious thing"! - Donara seemed to be perplexed. – You can speak? – asked the woman who seemed to be unable to tear herself from the young man. There was Mary coming up the stairs with a huge bag. He grasped her together with the bag and they both entered the flat silently.

I'm here, Data! – the warm voice made him come to his senses.

Come! – She thought she heard. She held her breath and then she embraced the man to make him sure that it was all the same for her.

[1] Daisi – Georgian folk dance the motives of which were used by Zakaria Paliashvili, famous Georgian composer in his opera of the same name.

My names Gozala, no kidding!

(Dedicated to my friend Nino)

Once upon a time there lived a woman. She was a well-to-do one. But now all of her acquaintances had turned into her creditors. All the relatives, friends and neighbors as well as co-workers had been looking for her. Each morning started with a telephone call. In the evening she had to receive visitors. She had some debts at the State Bank too.

She used to spend the money earned by her own labor at her discretion. And the discretion was quite strange. Money was somewhat of a necessity for her. And it did no matter who was the owner of the thing that she needed so badly. She did it whole-heartedly and no one had ever refused to get the sum offered by her. She helped everyone, strangers and relatives, close and remote ones if they were in need. She just handed round her fortune.

When someone asked her to lend him some money she even borrowed some if she had no some of her own. Then the debtors failed to give the money back for the indigence and she started to do almost the same over and over again. She looked for the way out of the situation, quelled the creditors and the debtors and finally found out that she was the only aggrieved person in the happening.

It was her character that people loved Leli for. They lauded her to the skies but the praise did not help her avoid the loss in the end. She sold the house and car and moved to a rented apartment but nothing had changed with respect to the high-percentage credit (there are too many money-lenders in the world).

Yes, it never rains but it pours. The economic crisis in the country reached its peak and the young woman with too many debts was left unemployed. And the creditors poured unanimously. The telephone didn't stop ringing - rang all the debtors, one after another. When she went somewhere to find some money for someone there was always a creditor waiting for her at home. That was something that seemed to have no end.

She beat for a way out and finally submitted an application form to the US Embassy. She hoped that an American salary would be a salvation. Oops! The application was refused. She turned her attention to Europe and tried to go to England. Though, she happened not to have the luck! In herown country it was impossible to get a job.

Thinking about the debts she didn't sleep on nights. It was the sense of responsibility that had made her so restless. It was a true sore point with her. Because of the answerability before the people she had to experience somewhat of a deep sorrow...The responsibility and the unsolved problems were just incompatible.

One morning she dressed up and went out. She stopped in front of the house and peered into the ground. Sometime there was a beautiful garden growing over there. In spring a flowering lilac spread its odor throughout the street. The recollection made her feel some joy. "How happy I used to be then. I had no debts... No, I just didn't know what it was like. And Sandro used to wait for me under the tree. While I blowing dry my hair he gathered lilac branches for me and gave me the bouquets on the stairs. We were surrounded by the smell of the flowers all day long. The thoughts stole up into Leli's mind.

All of a sudden she touched the earth. There were some weeds growing instead of the lilac. She tried to pass the anguish to the soil through her fingers. The emotion was so strong that she even felt the smell and she forgot the grief for a minute or so... A telephone ringer brought her back to the everyday problems. She did not even try to take the phone from her bag for she had nothing to tell the one calling her. She just went on.

She didn't know where she was going to. She stepped along the street supplicating to free her from the ordeal. Without noticing the traffic lights she instinctively quickened her steps. There was a true chain of cars at the crosswalk. Suddenly a black jeep appeared from the right. The preoccupied woman had no time to run away. The driver failed the car as well and stroke against her. Leli fell down right on her right foot. The driver rushed to her. The man who had got pale was looking down at Leli like a mad. Then he took her in her hands, put her into the car and drove her at full speed to the Ghudushauri Clinic.

There was a general alarm raised for the staff over there. The deputy Mayor of the City took the professor into a separate room and asked him to examine each organ. When she came to consciousness, Leli felt an ache in her flank. It came out that she had a bruise on the side.

She has to stay at the hospital for a while, - they said to Giorgi Tughushi. It goes without saying that the Deputy Mayor took upon himself all the treatment costs.

What's your name? - asked Giorgi when they were left alone in the ward. She felt a desire to open her heart to the man. The anxiety that she had been experiencing for years had shattered her peace and quiet. She looked up at the stranger with some confidence in her eyes and surveyed him shyly. – Why didn't I die she said to herself.

The words shocked the man. The young and beautiful woman wished to die. It was so incomprehensible for him. He wondered what the reason was but he didn't dare say something. Leli did not know who the man was. She took him for just an elegant one and told him about everything frankly. Giorgi listened to her with attention, though he didn't utter a syllable. He let her tell the story to the very end and when she stopped he looked closely at her face. It was too strange. He had never heard anything of the kind. A young woman having the beauty and the luxury had ruined her life just because she wanted others to be successful. What was it? Was it her nature? Enormous kindness or just foolishness...He was deep in though.

The man spellbound by the woman did not even try to make something out. Her sincerity and all the details of her life told without coloring the truth were quite enough for him to make a decision. He stayed at the clinic that night. The doctors persuaded him that it was not necessary for him to be there but he was not going to cross the threshold of her room.

The next day she told the man who had already got accustomed to her: - How could you strike me with the car? - They both laughed with a hearty laugh. He had lost his head. The charming and sad woman with a good sense of humor was too tender. She was so lovely when grieving over something and when she was glad.

Early in the morning he burst into the room and told her:

We'll go right to my place. I'll marry you. - Leli couldn't understand whether the man was kidding or not. – Maybe he is the one to solve the problems, - she thought first. She did not answer him. She remembered Sandro, the only man she had ever been in love with and shook her head.

Leli was discharged from the hospital. Giorgi Tughushi took her home. On their way home they talked much. Finally he told her who he was. She knew only the name of the Deputy Mayor. She got confused but gave no sign of the confusion.

Leli, let's go to your creditors! Go to them right now. Let me settle the problem for you. – He seemed to be too unfeigned.

Sorry, I cannot! – Leli cut short and opened the door. Then she leaned towards him and said:

Thank you for all you've done for me! Good-bye! – She walked with her hurried steps into the front door.

Shall I take my own life? – No – Maybe it would be better for me to run away? – She sauntered along the quay of the River Mtkvari with a worried expression of her face. She saw too many people crowded at a booth. She moved towards the kiosk to satisfy her curiosity. She looked at those standing in a queue with interest and listened to them. A middle-aged man told a young women standing just by his side that he had won a certain sum due to his lottery ticket. He also said that he was going to try his fortune again. Leli made a gesture meaning that she had given it up as lost and went on.

A gipsy woman cut off her way and started to talk with her trying to speak Georgian just as she could do it. – Dear, there has been a big sorrow kept in your heart. Why did you say "no" to him...listen! Three days and the grief will disappear. Aaah! Come to me then! I'm always here (she pointed to the entrance of the market). Gozalla, yes, Gozalla, it's my name.No kidding! Don't look at me this way. I'm not a lier. - Leli nodded automatically and continued to walk along the street. Then she opened a small purse. She had two coins there, a one-lari coin and a two-lari one. She ran after the Gipsy and gave her one lari. She paid two laris for a lottery ticket, quickly crossed out six figures and went home.

The moon lit the wan and sad face of the young woman standing on the balcony. She knew no rest for she had much to think about the debts. She did not accept the proposal of the rich and powerful man, though he could solve all the problems just in a day.

There was a commercial about shampoo on the TV – nonsense – she smiled bitterly and looked up at the sky. The stars were flashing like a happy one throughout the dim colors surrounding them. - I wish I were a star! - She thought and tears ran out of her eyes. They started a jackpot drawing. Leli remembered about something and looked into the room. She was a bit frightened. On a tiny pink leaf there were six figures stricken out. The small sheet could change her life in a jiffy. The middle-aged man was going to try again.

She set down comfortably at the TV. She was mute. The balls started to move. The anchorman announced the numbers marked on the colored balls following one another. She has crossed out all the figures – Was it possible? - Leli could not believe her eyes. The fifth ball did not make her wait for a long. She fell down on a long and narrow stripe. On the pink piece of the paper she had crossed the fifth figure too.

She could not see any more. There was no need to see something for it did no matter whether the sixth figure was going to coincide or not. It was enough, enough to pay off the debts. It was over, finally over! She remembered the Gipsy woman: three days and the grief will disappear! She broke away from the room and filled with feelings called the God from the balcony: "Thank God! Thank God"!

Leli made up all the debts and had a sigh of relief after the four years full of problems. She had just thirty laris left from the won sum. But that was the thing that she really wanted. She put on the clothes hurriedly and went to the market. It was not difficult to recognize the Gipsy. – Gozalla, come! - she called. Gozalla who seemed to be surprised tried to keep away. Then Leli came to her and put twenty-five laris into her palm. Gozalla pleased by the present called: Good girl! Beautiful girl! The woman left the place as if she was afraid of Leli who could take the money back.

Leli carrying a sum of just five laris passed along the avenue like seagull always flying so freely and easily... She had to cover a long way before reaching the house. She decided to have a cup of coffee at the café built right there. There were some young people gathered at the café. The entrance door stood wide open. There was a beggar sitting at the door. Suddenly she ran to the pauper. It was her heart calling her to do so. She smiled to the beggar and put the last five laris into his palm now. The man stood up. Yes, he was happy for he had to sit in the street to earn the sum for ten days. It was the nature and it was not a fault. "I'll do it again what has made me suffer too much. I can do nothing with it for I was born with it all". Blez Pascal once said: "impossible to be either eradicated or changed".

Leli went home. She was happy and untroubled and her heart was beating full of joy. She did not have a penny to her name and she had no debts. It had happened!

She felt someone touching her arm. He made her turn around. There was a man whom she wanted to see more than anyone else. She spread her hands and put her arms round his shoulders. Then she dropped her eyes down and said in a timid manner:

You know what?! I've never loved you so much!

It was your hair that helped me to recognize you, - said the boy and put his head onto her soft hair having the smell of the lilac so very familiar to them.

October 13

Nana jumped out of her bed as if someone had pushed her out of it. Her shoulder was aching. She put her palm on the forehead trying to remember something. She could not understand why the dream came to her so frequently. What does it mean? What's up with her? When she was thinking about the dream her mother came to her unnoticeably.

- It's early, honey! Why are you getting up? – Nana looked down at the clock. It was 06:40 AM. She did not answer and returned to the bed. No, she had no doubts that the vatic dream had some special meaning for her.

She saw a dream. She was walking up some stairs, upper and upper. When she had almost reached the last footstep a pigeon set down on her shoulder and started to coo. She failed to rid herself of the bird. A sweet melody was coming out of its tiny beak. She had seen the dream too many times. No, it's impossible to count. When she wakes up she hears the cooing and she feels the pleasant ache in the shoulder. It's the shoulder where the pigeon sits in the dreams.

It was impossible for her to attend the lectures. She asked a friend of hers to miss one and they followed the avenue. The bare trees grew along the sidewalk like lampion poles. The autumn had already disrobed the nature and the wind had been rocking the leaves to sleep. Nana told her friend about something and tears ran out if her eyes.

Just nine months had passed since the time when she was given birth. Her mother used to tell her about her childhood. It was amazing, but she could remember only the silhouette of her father. All the recollections were really dim… He was a tall, broad-shouldered man. His stature made it difficult for him to enter the door. When he came back from work she used to meet him at the threshold and ask him to take her into the arms. The man grasped the girl with his hands and caressed her. Then he sat down on a couch and started to untie the shoestrings. The small girl turned back as if she had remembered something and ran to the slippers with her teeny steps. She brought them to her father and put them down. Then she squeezed the huge shoe in her hands and took it away reeling from side to side. No one had ever told her to do that. It was her own idea, an idea of a clever and witty child.

The country had been warring against its enemies. Valodia was twenty-six years old and they called him up. He got ready, stopped at the door, stretched both hands to his wife to say good-bye, took her against his breast and asked her: please bring her up, take care of her and you'll see what can I do for you when I'll be back. He seemed to have forgotten that it was her daughter too.

Valodia went to Kerch. He had two companions: the thought about his family and the anguish. There was no one left in the village but women and children. In the evening little Nana as if waiting for her dad used to stand in the doorway till her mother took her to bed in her arms. The girl always cried then.

Nana tells her friend about her father and cries. She wants to have a dad tall and handsome like the man she can remember. And mom tells her about him from time to time. He was just twenty-six years old, too young and full of life.

The family had been waiting for him for a quite long period of time, though all in vain. When they got to know that that head of the family was not alive she was twelve years old. The elder ones had already started families of their own.

They chose a cozy nook at a small garden and sat down on a bench there. It was cool a little. Nana had beautiful amber beads around her neck. Nato liked the beads too much. Suddenly Nana put them off, came to Nato and said: - we are going to leave the institute this year. Let it be a keepsake. I'll be glad to see you with the beads. Nato refused first. Then she hugged her friend and thanked her with a heartfelt gratitude. Nana put the beads around Nato' neck herself and they stepped out of the public garden.

Two years passed. She went to work at school and got married. But she did not stop thinking about her father, about his ill fate and his life and the untimely death. She thought about everything associated with the man. Her kind heart was full of the sad memories and thoughts about the days spend in loneliness.

She often sees the stairs in her dreams feeling the pigeon sitting right on her shoulder and hears its cooing. When she wakes up she feels the pleasant and weird pain in her shoulder. She thinks about the dream coming to her as frequently as of something enigmatic.

She married an artist. The famous painter had too many spiritual values. In their idyllic family there always was an atmosphere of calmness. They received more and more guests each day. All the friends and relatives loved her. Anyone who had ever met her was fond of her.

A little girl was their firstborn. A boy was the second. They both were niveous and nice - two offsprings of the great artist and his small Nana.

All of a sudden the artist turned away from the ideal family. He forsook them without a word. He just closed the door…Nana who was taken aback remembered her father. They both left her. The difference was that her husband said nothing before going. Her father had to go to Kerch and it meant that he would never be back. They both did just the same. Though, they knew why her father was going to leave the family and the decision of her husband was a stunning blow.

Five years passed. The feeling of emptiness appeared to be so terrible, so agonizing that she unintentionally started to paint. She painted all days long. Maybe she had missed him or maybe it was an attempt to keep the emptiness in secret. It seemed to be a true way out and a miracle cure for all her pains. She painted all the time unlike the lonely women always searching for love. She had closed the door of her heart tightly and forever.

She painted anytime when she remembered the man. Landscapes, portraits and still lives were scattered on the tables. Finally she painted the dream: the stairs and its ending and the tiny bird sitting on her shoulder… The painting happened to be so realistic that she was surprised herself.

Probably she was waiting for the dream or something else to come true...She could not realize what the thing might be.

It was rumored that she had started to paint. One evening a friend of her husband's came to her place and suggested organizing an exhibition. Nana said that she was not a professional and refused the suggestion first but Devi who turned out to have forceful arguments managed to make her agree with him. He promised to settle all the things for her and told her about her husband who had been gone to Europe for four years. There was no one to know everything about the man.

The exposition hall was packed with people. In the evening when they were going to close the hall a man in strange clothes came and asked to let him in just for a jiffy. When he entered he was amazed by the works. The name of the artist made him embarrassed. He read: Nana Tskhvedadze. – Maybe it's not her? Or...- He dashed out of the exhibition hall.

Nana who has never painted a flower and could just be an admirer of the works of others had turned into a painter. It was a sign for Nikoloz, a sign having the all-embracing meaning. It was not the special talent that makes people paint, it was love. – The man walked along the street... He decided to see her. Nothing else could have calmed him down.

All absorbed in though he came out of the tube. Just thirty meters divided him from the place where Nana lived. It was the place that he had left without ceremony and without words. He walked up the stairs hurriedly and knocked against the door. No one was going to open it for him. He grasped the handle and the door opened. He stepped in and went to the table. He was dumbfounded and ashamed for he had clung to the paintings as if there was someone who was going to take them away. "Nana, my dear, Nana"! - repeated the man. Then he found some drink in the wall-cupboard and drank it at a gulp. He even fell asleep buried in the pictures.

It was a quiet evening in October and it was drizzling. Nana led her children home by the hand. The boy asked her to buy some ice-cream. She bought it for them both. When they came out of the shop she turned back, as if something had stricken her mind and bought a small cake packed in a box. It was October 13, her birthday. For some reason no one had remembered her this time. She is the only one who has not forgotten the date. She'll spread the table at home with all the fruit, and meat dish and wine. She'll cut the cake and tell her children once again that it's her birthday today.

The boy was the first one to run up the stairs. The girl went next to him. Nana followed them slowly. The unexpectedness made her torpid. The children folded in the arms of their father seemed to be too happy and glad. She looked at them quite long without being noticed. When the three saw her they all moved towards her with their hands reached out to her. The girl had burst into tears and mumbled jerkily: -Mom, dad has come! Mom! Dad, dad...- finally she could say nothing but the only word and she repeated it over and over again. The happiness had come to the family of the great painter...

That's great! That's great! – He looked smilingly right into her eyes. He had some paintings of his wife in his hands instead of some flowers. Her face was brightened with the feeling of happiness that she had never experienced before. She thought he had come to say happy birthday to her and she was glad that he had not forgotten about the day.

But his congratulations were all about the predestination that she was going to be a great artist herself. For the man it was a token of the love that he failed to appreciate. Now it was the time for him to feel regret, the time that necessarily comes to each person.

Nikoloz had rested his head upon her shoulder just like the resting pigeon from her dreams.

The moonlight lit the window glasses and there was a fire even bigger than the moon burning in their children's eyes.

Its your ghost

In the yard of a tiny house built right in the thickness of the forest an old woman carrying a candle was looking at the Sun and senselessly gazed around herself. One might think that the woman was looking for someone there. Having had already got used with the loneliness she bustled silently as if she was angry. The sixty-seven-years-old woman could neither read nor write. She had never gone to school. She had had problems with the eyesight since her childhood and could not see clearly, though she new each corner perfectly and could do the housework even with the eyes closed.

You'd quite often see her with a candle in her hand. It was somewhat of a rite accompanied by the traces of childhood and the thirst. Her ancestors often lighted candles. Several times each day she took a candle and walked hither and thither with it. Sometimes she burnt the tapers.

Two or three times a month she visited her neighbor living on the slope. She used to sit down on a stump there and God knows which time told about the past in short phrases so very habitual for her.

The significance of the past days had made her loose the sense of the present time. Yes, she had nothing to think about the present that had totally disappeared from the consciousness. She did not even have an idea of the fact that her village was the highest settlement from the sea level in Europe.

Kesso and Kato were twin sisters. There was a long, long century left before the civilization reached the part of Georgia where they lived. The Great Patriotic War had marked families much wealthier than their own one. They were three years old when the twins suffered from German measles. The aftereffects of the illness took Kato's life. Kesso recovered from the disease comparatively easily. The parents mourned over the dead child, though the flow of time and the care taken after Kesso made them pick up from the grief.

She was beautiful but she knew nothing about her beauty. People talked much about her appearance. If they caught a sight of her, they started the endless talks about the girl.   She was the most beautiful woman in whole Svanetia. When she got 28 unexpectedly died her father. Soon afterwards departed her mother too.

Kesso was left alone. Years passed fast in silence and the old age sneaked up to her. The youth and the years of loneliness were dim and faded out.

Her visits to the neighbor got more frequent. Every other day she set in her yard. The neighbor feeling pity for Kesso, treated her, talked with her and saw her off through the road.

Kesso, who had never gone to school and never took part in the gatherings held in the village, hurried to Mariam with an expression that seemed to be so very businesslike.

She had never seen a TV set and had never been to the local club where a silent film was shown. The neighbor used to be her own TV, the lightship of her partially blinded eyes, the mirror and the radio. She had never experienced happiness greater than the visits and she could never imagine the beatitude of life greater than the latter.

It was in May. Kesso put on her grey summer dress. Her face was shone with joy of meeting the neighbor. Her perfect face had turned pink. The thirty-eight-years-old woman had hid the graceful oval of her face. She went up the rise. A sunny smile was covering her features.

The neighbor saw Kesso from the balcony of the first floor. "Wait for a moment", - said the woman and pointed to the chair standing on the balcony. When she approached the door she took a glance of a stranger through the curtain of her weak eyesight. She had never seen the person. Kesso grew torpid. She took her hand to the face and turned her back to the unknown woman. Then she stealthily looked towards the stranger again. The staring woman woke up her curiosity. She could not understand who the stranger might be.

Kesso stepped back and looked aside. The ghost did not seem to have any intention to move from there. It was looking right into her face. Kesso was rather perplexed. She fell down of the chair…but it was curiosity again that rose questions in her mind about the stranger and about the reasons that the ghost had for looking at her so fixedly.

Suddenly she put her hand on the forehead as if something has reminded her about itself. She smiled and thought that the stranger could have been her twin's ghost. In her imagination the ghost wore the same grey frock and the same shoes. She remembered her mother's words about her twins always dressed equally. Even their hair was plated identically then.

Mother told her that Kato was as beautiful as her sister. And now the twin sister was standing in the depth of the room slightly aloof from her. Because of her eyesight she could not realize whether it was an apparition or a silhouette of a real being standing there in the door opening.

The appearance of her own ghost made Kesso happy and full of odd thoughts. In confusion she was not able to understand what were the things going on, though she was obviously willing to get nearer. Still experiencing some fear she preferred to sit silent and keep observing the image.

Mariam's voice made her sober up. Mariam sat by her side and started to talk. Kesso answered her in a manner that was quite confused. She wondered why the woman did not notice the ghost of her twin sister and why she said nothing about it. She looked at her sister again. Kato's look was just a copy of her own one. Kesso waiting for the phantom to talk to her kept silent on the chair. She could not catch the essence of what the presage was about.

Mariam was amazed by Kesso's strange gaze and gestures but she decided to make no sign.

Grandma told Kesso that embodied souls of relatives can really come to a person. But why in the very house…There was no one to tell about the anxiety troubling Kesso so much.

When she came home she did not stop thinking about Kato. She could not forget the amazed face looking at her like a ghost. She was eager to go to the neighbor again, wanted to see the image and ascertain whether it was a soul, an embodied angel or just a shook.

She spent a year visiting her neighbor from time to time. She used to sit down right there where it was easier to see the ghost, though she did not dare to say anything. She also could not understand why the twin sister observing her on the sly stood up and took her leave simultaneously with Kesso.

The New Year came. Kesso made up her mind to go to the neighbor again. She put on some special clothes. From the old wardrobe she took the warm fur coat not yet worn. It had been hung there for years. She put the dark kerchief knitted by her mother on too. In the mountainous village it was rather cold. That day she decided to touch the image at any price. Full of joy and decision she went to Mariam.

A countrywoman met her. Astonished Lili had never seen Kesso so prettily dressed. Kesso hurried up to avoid questions. Lili followed Kesso with her eyes and said: "poor, poor Kesso, she has gone maid". The woman shook her head with regret and went on.

Kesso hurried to Mariam's yard. It was not easy to hide the impatience. Sometimes it was impossible even to understand what she was talking about. Finally the petulance revealed itself. She could not stand the moment of waiting before talking with the ghost.

Mariam went up to the first floor to see the sleeping grand-child. Kesso leapt the opportunity and stood up in another heartbeat with the heart beating too roughly. Feelings of fear and joy were mixed together. Just a meter, just two steps and they'll be side by side… she heard some crashing noise and felt a pain in her legs that she had never suffered before. She almost stopped breathing and glancing around the room fell down as if she had steeped into a deep slumber. When she recovered she saw that the ghost had already disappeared. There was just a grey wall instead of the image. Her small, skinny legs were aching.

Mariam who had heard the noise had readily come. Kesso was lying down on the floor and the pieces of the tocher mirror were scattered at her legs.

Marian looked down at Kesso uttering some words with a vacant stare. "Where, why, Kato",- repeated the woman with her eyes closed. She seemed to be even angry with the sister's ghost who had refused to be with her.

Many years passed and many things changed in the every-day life of the village. Kesso who is seventy-seven years old now neither sits in the yard nor visits Mariam. She just sometimes comes out from the yard, shades her hand over the face and looks towards some unknown direction.

The most beautiful face has already turned into wrinkles. Her eyes partially able to see things around her look at the path leading to the neighbor's house built on the hill. The state of mind shall never let her go up the slope again.

The thing is that Kesso had never seen a mirror before.

1787 Posters

Dedicated to my daughter Eka, who was
hopelessly in love with the football star – David Backham.
She was eleven years old then.

(Based upon real facts)

The daydreamer who was eleven years old then watched a football match. She sat by the side of her father and she was the very image of his. The large maroon eyes were sparkling. The long and straight hair and the lovely nose made the childish expression so very nice.

She was so calm and delicate that it was hard for anyone not to hold her in respect. She could easily remind one of a person with a clear mind. She was so polite and courteous, so naïve and sensitive. All the excessive emotions kept inside her sometimes needed to be brought out of her heart.

They were alone in the room: she and her father. The quietness and the unusual harmony together with the festive mood that had set over there made me go out of the room silently. They were waiting for the final victory by the end of the match.

Suddenly I heard someone crying in a loud voice. One of the soccer players had scored a goal. She had sprung to her feet and was clapping her hands joyfully. She looked at her father with those kind eyes, put herself against his breast and bounced up and down. Then she turned to me and said: - Mom, come! Look at it! What a goal it was. It was him who scored it, - she pointed her finger—to the screen. Soon they announced the name of the boy who had made the goal. It was David Backham. Her small heart just shivered. She had heard the name and she knew that he was the best. The excited girl jumped and repeated and repeated: - Mom, look, how handsome David Backham is!

The goal had made her so glad that one might have though all the childhood dreams had already come true. She twittered and giggled and hugged her dad. It was an indescribable joy. I looked at her all surprised. I've never seen her so happy and rapturous. She was not so happy even when we celebrated her fifth birthday and she got all the toys that she wished to have.

The supper had already been served. I called the two from the kitchen. Though, none of them could hear me calling. When I entered the room they were watching the match with such an attention that I just gave up and stepped out. There was no use in calling them.

Later the noise made by the father and his girl made me know that it was Backham's team who'd won. She leapt up and was almost bawling. She was in raptures. Her father, her confederate was by her side. He was also shining with joy sharing the gladness of the girl.

When I came in she moved towards me. She told me about the team's victory and could do nothing with the anxiety and happiness. She seemed to have found a man she had been looking for with her childish underself. His athletic achievements had made him a true hero in her eyes. And the hero had gained general acceptance. The godsend had made her glad and full of life.

She did not get a wink of sleep that night. The thoughts about him did not give her a moment's peace. She saw the fair-haired youngster with the glittering eyes that were full of mischief. And his smile was so wonderful. The imagination reflected all the images of the silhouette, his supple running round the field, the tiny and delicate nose and the amazing teeth that he used to show off when he was tired. Then she heard that the blond man was the captain of the team. It was another point in his score. He got greater and greater, shining like a huge and transparent star burning over there in the sky.

I was her mother and I wanted to know what was going on in the soul of my child. Though, she used to be sincere just when we were watching TV. Any other time she prepared to keep silent. Hence, all I'm going to tell you now is about my daughter's life that I had to witness when we lived under the same roof.

Eka secretly gathered information about him. The matches on the TV got more and more frequent. Some of them were showed at three or four o'clock at night (local time). I repeated over and over again that it was unhealthy for a little girl to sit up the nights. But she never gave it up. When we were all asleep she used to get up noiselessly from her bad and sat down at the TV. She watched the matches and her beloved one, her hero, her knight used to make a goal after another.

Football was idolized in our city. Dinamo Tbilisi was a powerful and recognized team when I was a child. Today the information obtained by football fans about their favorites is even richer than it has ever been. All the posters, papers and magazines with the articles about them are sold everywhere, in shops and booths. I saw the pile of the posters growing each day in size on Eka's table. She wanted everything to the last penny to buy another placard with a picture of Backham's.

Almost everyone in the school and in the suburb knew about her love towards the man. Her friends used to come to our place each holiday and brought his images to her. She decorated her bed-room with the pictures. The papers running the truth and the rumors about Backham were scattered on the table. In the entrance and on the facade walls someone had written "DAVID BACKHAM" with chalk.

She could answer any question about the man. She learned that he saw Victoria when he was watching TV in a hotel room; and they fell in love with each other there.

Once when I was tidying up the rooms to get rid of the unnecessary things kept in the cupboards and drawers I came upon a huge pile. It was too heavy for me to be picked up. I could not understand what it was. In a large transparent bag I found too many paper sheets folded up. I was just amazed. I opened the bag and saw all the clippings with Backham's photos and articles about him. They were put together so carefully that the picture made me really thoughtful. There were too many cuttings. When and where did she manage to gather all the stuff?

A few years passed. Eka got fifteen years old and the only thing that she used to ask about was a sum of money that was enough to buy another poster. It seemed she had never had any other goal.

The information about two new books by Backham already on sale reached us too. She sought for any piece of news about the books but her close friend Marrie passed ahead of us and made a present to her: a full version of the books. There seemed to be no limits to her happiness. She clasped her friend and put the precious gift to her breast. Her eyes were sparkling with happiness.

It took her a week to read the book. I heard her telling her friend: - Marie, I did not know Backham was so unpretentious.

One day I came home and saw my girl with her friend Tamuna sitting together in the room. Under the posters with the pictures of Mr.Backham there was a modest table spread with an obvious feeling of expectation: some chocolate bars and liqueur and a small, lovely cake… There were three wine glasses standing under the posters too. When she saw me, she raised her glass and said: - mom! It's his birthday today. The second day of May…Long live to the best footballer and the most handsome man in the world! - And she drank it at a gulp. She looked up at Backham's posters with her eyes glittering so strangely.

The years of the hopeless love elapsed. The girl who was sometime just eleven years old had already got sixteen. She spent her time in front of the mirror parting her hair in the middle or just at one side. Sometimes she gathered her hair at the top and looked into the glass. One might have thought that she was coquetting with somebody. Though, all her thoughts were only about the man, David Backham.

Among the posters pasted to the wall you could even see some pictures of his spouse Victoria. On one picture she had put on a wonderful dress, on another she was attending a football match and had jumped up to her feet. She loved her for the woman was the chosen one of the man she had been considering to be the most handsome and popular man throughout the world.

It was the happiest day in her life when we heard that Real was going to arrive in the Tbilisi. She was more than happy. She thanked the God for making her dreams come true. The stadium stood right in front of our house and she'd see him, the man that she'd been longing for over there. She had a chance to really witness the goals scored by him and she'd see his charming smile just in thirty meters from her house.

She even bought some special clothes for the day. We went from a shop to another together with her friends looking for something original. Finally she got some rare jeans, a pair of white sneakers and a white cap. She put all the clothes on and appeared before her friends. They met her with applause and said that everything was just fine.

She had made up a plan: she wanted to meet him at the exit and tell him about her passion for him. She was going to invite him to our place and show him the room where she had spent all the years together with her childish dreams. To tell him everything as it was she learned English just zealously. She knew all the new words and expressions.

She lost sleep over the days to come. She thought about David Backham running thought the Tbilisi Stadium. She counted the days on her fingers. It was like a bolt from the blue when she heard that it was just a rumor and Real was not to come to play in Tbilisi...It was painful for her...She was always sad then. She used to take her eyes away from us and cried without saying a word...

Two more years passed. The recollections of the wrecked match always made her gloomy. Then she tried to get in contact through the net. Though, she realized that all the efforts were useless. It made her say goodbye to all the hopes.

Four years later she got twenty. Now she studies at the University and attends the lectures. She always tells her brother that he is to be a football player as popular as Backham. She takes him to the coachings herself. She is his fan and the one who encourages him. The boy is twelve years old and does his best for he loves and obeys his sister.

One day she saw a blond boy on the moving staircase of an underground station. She ran down the stairs quickly, passed ahead of him and looked at him from the front. He was the image of Backham. She smiled automatically and said what she had been willing to say for years:

My God! Is that you? - She asked in English. The boy smiled. It was not the first time he was given the question.

No, dear, I am not Backham. – He said in Georgian. – I'm Pako. I don't like soccer. I'm a musician and I can write a nice song for you. – He seemed to have liked the girl and started a conversation with her. She joined him in the chat and they passed their way talking joyfully. Soon she realized that the reality and the dreams had little in common. The dreams had turned into attempts to feel what it is like to experience happiness. They were wonderful, though – impossible. And besides, the reality that appeared to be so good and staggering was much better.

They met each other several times. They even made friends with each other. When Pako goes on tour she calls him and they talk.

"My Bax", - that's how she calls him. The infatuation of the child now seems to have turned into something real. I think the passion for the man was caused by the discovery of her own ideal.

I asked her how many pictures of Backham were there in her collection. She said that she had 1787 of them. Some of them were set in a frame, others papered on the walls or cut out of the press. The resemblance makes her think that it's Pako looking down at her from the wall carrying a ball in his hand instead of the guitar. And besides, she can hear his wonderful voice singing right by her side.

And still, which one? - I asked cautiously. "Bax is the only one" – she said and it was a sign for me that the Backham from the reality was rather special...

The boy of bamboo

His thinness could easily make one think that he had never had a bite. He was thin and strangely lowly. God knows how many wishes he had but it was his reticence that helped him to keep the wishes in secret. No one knew what the thoughts that made the youth act were.

He was tall and wagged his long legs like bamboo canes when walking. He used to dance sometime. He could sing and was a perfect drummer. He knew Georgian and Russian poetry almost by heart. His mother did her best to grow him up as a learned man having good manners. Though, his father was a hard drinker and a true bully. He used to drink all the time and made too much trouble. He was divorced with his first wife and when he unburdened his heart bickering with the woman and her son he used to run to the has-beens to continue the wrangle and just to go back again. Maybe he was the reason that had made Nugo reserved. But he never spoke about and it was almost impossible to talk to him about too. He did not like to talk about himself and share his opinions most of all. When someone asked him:

Nugo, do you think that's right?—he always hung his head down as if thinking about the answer with his breath bated. He would say his lesson and recite poetry for you but he would never tell you a word about himself and the things that he used to think over.

He left school and was called up for military service. It was a real misfortune for him. The skinny body looked so ridiculous in the military uniform with the jackboots. He was appointed a prison guard there and if any of the prisoners tried to escape he had to shoot at him immediately. Even a brawl was a problem for the honest and fair boy and now he was to fire a rifle. Wounding somebody's feelings was somewhat of a fatal mistake for him. He could not understand why he had to hurt others. - What's that? – he said, - are we given birth just to grapple with each other though it? – It was his world-view that he never talked about. One could just feel what his ideas were about.

He would never treat anyone badly and it was impossible for him to kill anyone. He was just forced to speak up and that was the very first case when he enunciated his point of view. He opposed the master sergeant and threw it right into his face: - No, I'll never shoot, I'll never do that even if you kill me, - Nugo raised his voice. The courteous bamboo boy suddenly changed.

The instruction ran counter to his humane nature and he tried to protect himself from the guilt.

In the army a soldier is not the one who predetermines the fortunes over there. No regular can decide the fortune of the country as well. There are some specific laws and rules working in the army and no one needs nether neither a heedful heart nor a kind nature. Everyone has to obey the orders and keep hidden his own philanthropic ideas. He took his place at the watch with a tommy gun. But he did it just to deceive the command. He had no intention to shoot.

You must shoot at the jail-breakers, - he heard Molotov's voice and all in melancholy stood over there on the roof of the prison. The boy with his bamboo legs spent the sleepless nights standing at the watch-box and wished that no one would ever try to run away. He was so strongly fond of life and so very tired of the winter cold.

One night when he was on the roof again he caught forty winks. It was after midnight and he was still asleep. A sudden alarm made the buildings shake. When he jumped up he saw the chief of the unit moving towards him and crying in a loud voice:

Shoot at him! Damn it! Shoot! – Nugo looked at Kazantsev with his eyes full of supplication and then turned to the escapee who had already run quite far from the jail. The situation was so hopeless that he nearly fell down on his knees. He did not know what to do. Kazantsev grasped his shoulders and shook him too strongly that the staggering boy closed his eyes. He started to shoot with his eyes still closed. Some of the bullets were shot right into the air. The projectiles following one after another fell down with the droning sounds. He didn't even dare look in the direction and kept shooting with his eyes screwed up. He thought if he closed his eyes tight he would miss the mark and the prisoner would safely leave the territory.

Shortly after that Kazantsev approvingly stroke Nugo's shoulder and said: - You did well, Chavchavadze! – Nugo realized that notwithstanding all the attempts the projectile had shot the prisoner down. He threw the gun away with grief, hid his face into his palms and cried. He could hear how the wounded was taken to the prison hospital and put his hands on the ears. The horror had made him come to hate the life.

In the morning the commander thanked Nugzar Chavchavadze for his heroic effort, declared him a selfless soldier and handed a letter of commendation. Nugo threw the letter into a wastepaper basket and left the place without permission.

What a cheek! How did he dare! – Roared Molotov and commanded that he should be imprisoned. It was all the same for Nugo. He was ready for the most severe punishment. He hated himself for what he had done. He worried about the man at the hospital that he had wounded. Maybe he was not even alive.

They made him bide his time in prison for a month then he was released and told that drastic measures should be taken against him during the period of his military service. Nugo hung his head down again as a sign of obedience and thought: I have to see the wounded at any cost right this night. He knew the ward. It was the first window to the east of him. Even more, he knew that the man was wounded in the head.

It was half past two at night when he got up. He put on the clothes silently and opened the door. There was such a quiet in the exit that he could hear his own breathing. He did not think about the results. He did not care about himself. He had to see the prisoner and it was above all. It took him just ten minutes to pass the way. The guards seemed to be deep asleep. He noiselessly stole up to the fence. When crawling up the wall and jumping down from it he moved his bamboo legs so adroitly that he was surprised himself. When he came to the window and looked through it he thought about something…the idea could strike only a boy sensitive like him. "What can I tell him…make excuses? That does no matter…and I cannot… (He had never talked about himself)… thinking about it all he pushed the window that fortunately happened to be open. He crept through it silently and had a sigh just when he touched the floor with his feet. In the slightly lighted room he saw a boy sitting on his bad with his head bandaged. He was looking at him.

Как чувствуеш, брат?[1] – He threw himself upon the boy and put him against his breast heartily. Nugo was shivering.

Oh, my head…- cried out the wounded in Georgian. Nugo stepped back…

You are Georgian, man? – He looked into the boy's face all in surprise.

Yes, I'm Georgian. – Said the boy and added a bit later: That splitting headache…

So much the worse! – breathed out Nugo and stepped aside. He could hardly breathe because of the feelings of sorrow and despair.

That's not the most important thing…I'll return to Tbilisi soon…I have been missed it… my head…

Yes, I have missed it too. I'll be free in five months.—It was the second time in his life when Nugo said something about himself.

Suddenly the wounded boy turned to him, looked into his face and told him in a loud voice:

They let me out, brother! I'm mad, mad. – He put his hand on his bandaged head. – I've a "white chit". They never arrest us, you know? – He said as if he wanted to make his guest glad for him.

Really… I'm sorry. Hanging it's too good for me…- Nugo looked down into the earth and whispered: too good for me…Why I listened to Kazantsev, - the prisoner didn't hear the words and continued:

Sorry?! Sorry for me to go out? What's your name? Irakli? Yes, Irakli. It's the name of my friend. We were boys when we made friends with each other. Now he lives in Switzerland. I saw him in Tbilisi before they arrested me. He had arrived in Tbilisi then. I had to do time in prison for twelve years. I killed a man…You know whom?... My own dad… He used to beat mom…I could not forgive, man…Twelve years, it's too much, isn't it? Now they're going to release me. Freedom…It's a good thing. My love has been waiting for me in Tbilisi. – Nugo listened to the man and could not believe. "He talks over things quite normally. Really mad"?! – He looks at the wounded in the wide-eyed astonishment.

Long live to the soldier…Long live! He shot at me from the roof. Nice, he shot me right into my head. Long live! – The boy flaps his hands up in the air joyfully. I am free…Do you know what happiness is? Oh, my head… - suddenly he turned to Nugo and said:

Sorry, brother! Sorry! I have asked you nothing about you. Do you have a girlfriend? – The question made Nugo think over something. He remembered a dancing lesson, his classmate, and the girl who went in for dancing with him. At the concert he danced "Tseruli". Elene clapped so long and strongly that the audience noticed her. He loves her, he has been in love with her since the time, but no one knows about the love.

Nugo left the question unanswered… There is another ting that he is troubled about now. He does not know what to do…Tell him that it was him who shot then… Maybe it's better to keep it in secret.

[1] Как чувствуеш, брат? – (Russian) How are you, man?

34

The longed-for bareness of my soul

(My own Biography)

The sun was lighting the crystal vase so very gracefully that it made me experience a perfect feeling of joy. I stood up and started to pace almost instinctively. I could feel the happiness and loneliness at the same time. Generally speaking, I am a cheerful person less aware of a grief or sorrow. The melancholy does not stay with me long, just until the invasions of the uncontrolled optimism begin. And the rioting confidence has already marked my existence, you know. If the life has not been so full of indifference and troubles I would have been driven into apathy and the happiness set aside for me would have gone to someone else.

It's the Almighty who saves me. It's his love. He endowed me with the love, with the soul that is never cast down and with the Sun. I can't do without the Light. I'm sad without it burning for me for I'm always cold. I cannot stand the coolness even more than others. And those doleful thoughts start crawling into my mind. It's not my fault. It's just the nature and its inscrutable rule that makes me out of humor. The sadness prevails over me. Though, all of a sudden the optimism comes back and the hopes tied to the way leading to the goal attract me like a magnet. All covered with the rays of the Light, all entranced by the picturesque scenes, I can frisk and laugh endlessly for there have been all the wishes of mine already granted. That's the crest, the peak of my happiness.

It was cold. I was given life in the forbidding mounts in March. I was so helpless. When the senseless eyes of a newborn child were busy studying the world around them I just caught cold. That was the very start of the struggle with the life. The sickness and the strength to fight were inseparable. Hence, the strength seemed to be useless then for I was too young and silly to know all the methods of application.

The birth and the struggle for existence are nearly the same. Later on I accomplished the mission, but with some faults, sure. The roles assigned to the soul and body differed and it was impossible to make the couple work for one and the same reason. If one of them developed the other was always blocked. Years passed forcing the soul stay aside from the flesh. I was to make a choice between the two prospects: concerning myself with the soul or satisfying my physical needs. I was between the devil and the deep blue sea.

I don't know what the thing with the others is, how they manage to do all the things at the same time and do they really manage, but it was obvious I could never do the same. Even when I was old enough, I thought that all the material wants of a human being were settled down without any interference of his. As for the soul and its needs, I believed I had to work hard to appease them. Harmful to my health I happened to pay less attention to it and I really fell ill. My health was broken till I got even older.

The human happiness lies in doing things one is willing to do. And I was a slave of my likings. The thralldom of the kind was the only thing that made me bear the resemblance to the rest of the humankind. Though, all the dreams and thoughts of mine had less in common with the reality. My targets were almost unfeasible for the unknown virtues of the inner world had always been trying to do the opposite of the goals. Maybe years of wishful thinking are somewhat of a torment for others, but that was not the case with me. It was strange but the dreams made me just happy.

None of the reveries had come true and the novelties, even the longed-for ones, made me threatened and worried. The happiness and the greatest bliss of mine were the dream-like illusions all for my good. They lacked the pain and sorrow the fear of which had probably made me choose the odd state. Believe me, I was quite small when I realized that all the achieved dreams were accompanied by a certain pain. It was my delicate heart that I could not sacrifice to the pain.

I never remembered that I had to eat something or have my rest. I did not even sleep normally. My parents and my elder brothers had always been too kind to me. I used to read books all night long and I spent the days sitting and dreaming in my room. I just adored the moments of dreaming when I could wander throughout the made-up stories. And each time I thought it was impossible to experience the comfort again.

I was a really poor eater. My parents used to take me to different docs. They gave me all the vitamins and juices but they could do nothing with the small constitution. I just hated bread. When I saw my sister taking a bite of it I always felt some aversion. - How can she have it? It's so strange, - I thought and pulled faces.

When one does not take care of his health it's his nearest and dearest who try to do their best to help him. They had made too many promises to make me have a snack but there could be no promise to force me to eat. When I saw the food brought to me I got furious. Chocolate was the only thing that I really liked. They did not allow me to each too much I always had some hidden in my school-bag. I seemed to be willing to obey and I was self-willed. I seemed to be calm and modest, though I was not going to give up the voyages throughout the beautiful dreams. My soul was free and mighty and it never failed to keep the weak body in obedience.

The beauty of the mounts where I was brought up till I reached some age had marked the mind of the little daydreamer. With the lapse of time I realized that I belonged to the beauty, to the striking nature radiating the buoyancy. And we passed through the life always together and always side by side, me and the mounts, me and the Sun, me and the aeon and its shining beginning.

Yes, it would have been hard enough to find the same moral anywhere else in the world. The twinkles are always promising, though the distance between the fabulous future and the reality is too long. And besides, I have always been glad to find myself dancing the round dance with the facts that have never been challenging. I have never been busy enough and that is the reason.

The pain experienced by the soul used to touch the body. I suffered from different diseases from time to time. I had to have them all for I was careless and refractory and had my fate already sealed. That does no matter now. Now the cause cannot be subject to a judgment. There are really no people responsible for what has been going on.

It was my habitual pose to lie down on the back. And I used to think in the pose about the life and all the possible kind words that could make wonders and save one's future in a twinkling of an eye. I thought about the Sun shining in the distance. The passion to the Light and its heat had made me believe that the Sun was only mine. I thought it could belong to a girl in the universe rising in the transparent offing just to warm me. I was sure there was no one under the skies who could love it more than me or just like me.

I don't know what was it that made me write about my own self. There were actually no motives for the decision. It happened naturally and without taking the concepts into consideration. All the unfeigned talks and the moments of a different lifestyle pay heed neither to the expectations nor to the taste of a reader. Everything granted by the nature is good for its being free and easy. I talk to you as if you were all my friends. I'll tell everything I have to say to a friend of mine. Even a few sincere words are worth saying for they always help to keep in touch with the origins of mine, with my people and, of course, with you, my dear.

Maybe I'll repeat some of the phrases and I want to beg your pardon for that beforehand. I was alone and the loneliness was the thing that really kept me on for I had to get rid of the reality. That was the most essential condition for my inner resources to be realized. I'm sorry if you consider me to be a queer one. I'm sorry if the story makes you involved in all the odd things. Be lenient with me, please! Take it as a fact, as your own heartfelt words that you're eager to be understood by a reader. And besides, the lines are not written to glorify neither perfidy nor hypocrisy. They are not meant to serve the malicious intents of others.

It's good when people understand you, so very good that it makes you open your heart to let the happiness in. I had a few chances to experience the joy. And I cherished the beatitude like the dignity of my own always seeking for a soul similar to mine that I could accept and give the eternal shelter together with my heart.

My soul had its sea and the sea was dull. My soul had its mounts and green meadows spread with motley flowers…There were too many things so very desired and necessary for the existence. Maybe the things were, say, ordinary, but they had gathered all in a different dimension. Only a soul with some similar stories could do the sum. It just had to overstep the logical lines and deviate from the course called subsistence.

We must admit that any first lie is a way out from an unpleasant situation. It's an attempt to put oneself right to somebody. Step by step, little by little it turns into a habit. Yes, it's a habit and not an objective. It was uncommon but it happened that I had to deny the truth and prove a lie. Though, I was the most truthful when I told lies. It was my liberty, my freedom and they took it for a fault. You know, the doctrine of necessity is a thing about almost any event but it cannot be justified whenever you wish. I often preferred to keep silent for I did not want to play a false note. Though, I realized there was no one to understand me. I did not want to unobscure the enigmatic world of mine and the obsessions that had been so unthinkable for others just to secure myself. There is no one really eager to find himself in the strange chaos coming together with the feeling of inscrutability. It was my individual liberty that made me non-compliant in the fight with my own self. And it was my shyness relating to the genetics that prevented me from acting in the manner that I wanted to act in. As for the special respect for others, it was something running in my blood.

Notwithstanding the unusual silence and dissembled emotions I still managed to capture the attention of the people surrounding me. Always in conflict with the mysterious virtues I had to be taught all the lessons about audacity that would have necessarily helped me in avoiding oppression. I knew they did not understand me and managed to be so violently calm. And the expression of my face was so modest. I had always been sitting in the shade and there had never appeared a sign of objection. Maybe you think that keeping in the background is an awful thing that can fall to the lot of someone really unlucky. It is not necessary to stand in the foreground with one's neck stretched out to be successful or have a promising future, I think.

Remaining in the shadow was somewhat of expressing the unassuming attitude towards the people around me. That was the self-conscious nature that called me for having the stand. They complimented the little girl for her shyness and rebuked her at the same time. However, there were some people loving me even as I was. I had never made an attempt to put myself up for show. It was my wide reading unusual for the age that I could parade and there was nothing else but the reading. My parents tried to make me bolder, though they just failed. I could do nothing with the nature. I have already told that there was another state of mine, the loneliness and I was free and bold in the state, I was my own master there.

When the pleasing sounds produced by swallows could be heard from somewhere nearby and the earth warmed by the adorable Sun was fragrant with the cyclamen smell, when I was happy to experience only the giddy splendor of spring and the rhythm of the familiar melody used to steal through my soul. The beautiful billow made just a moment of the greatest bliss disobeying the rules of the time and taking its place in my heart with the obstinacy so very characteristic of it.

It happened in autumn. I sat at the window that evening looking up at the sky. It was blue as usual and there was nothing about the season that could make it different from any other autumn. I was in a queer mood. Now I think it was a bit early for the girl of seventeen to brood over the unfathomable ideas. The made-up universe and the real life pulled me down into the abyss of uncertainty and discord. The reality used to torture me almost every time when I had to make a step in my life. I could not accept it; I could not habituate myself to what had been going on. The two controversial things caused a complete chaos and a true outbreak inside me. Each unsolved problem dragged a brand-new one after it and pushed my tender heart together with the mind down to the emptiness, vacuousness of the human existence.

And I really wondered how people managed to succeed in their double dealing. Where did they hide their real faces?! The questions left without adequate answers have been shattering my peace since the time. It was a cold and cloudy day in March when the desire to settle everything down came to me. I was given birth that day. I started to explore the space around me with the eyes that were really naked then. I don't know why they had to say that the tiny being had no chances to lead a life of a self-sufficient one later on till the Creator decided to take me like a precious treasure of the nature with all my features and values. I was passed to the Lord in the Highest.

In the elementary school I took the world for a paradise. Though, the sensation had nothing in common with the reality. And the people looked like angels then. I was glad to be alive and thought I was a lucky one. I never believed that there could be any ill-wishers and considered the stories about them to be composed like all the fairy tales with their bad guys. And the tales seemed to be written for fun only. When I got older I took in that the people were just in front of me walking hither and thither all inspired and unaware of the fact that they had been violating all the canons of the Lord. I was a child unwilling to get used with the reality and declaring war on the secular rules. I used to build up all the relationships to help others live in a complete harmony and take delight in just living.

When I realized the possibility to pass away without having met anyone to understand me, I decided to write about my thoughts. It was snowing. I don't know whether the day was happy or unhappy for me, though I knew for sure that I did not have much in common with the snow-clad view but the indifferent and innocent gaze.

I wrote a poem, then I wrote another and in a month period I wrote around two hundred rhymes. Each syllable of the verses directly or indirectly indicated all the worries and thoughts of my own. I turned into a poet all of a sudden. No one had ever read or seen the poetry. (I'm sorry, but I really don't consider them to be poets who have already been introduced to the society, who have already published too many of their collections and who are often mentioned along with all the counterparts of their own. A poet living inside a human being shall never die till he can write a book. It's his poetic beginning and the nature that takes him to the reader). I used to write neither to produce an effect nor to be well-known. I was just driven by the inner virtue insisting on demonstrating what had been swollen up.

I'm afraid I can miss the most important thing, the greatest gift for love. It was as strange as I was. The thoughts coming out of my head like the sun-rays had got someone to be in love with. And the one was a forerunner of the joyful day that anyone looks for through the years of his life.

The one knew nothing. My alter ego appeared to be the most loyal friend of mine. The person that I happened to find inside me was too compassionate and less romantic. When I was too soft-hearted my friend used to rebuke me for it and taught me how to go through the sorrow. It told me how to be with the person having some ill intentions. It was such a protection and I was always dying to meet the friend like the best sister in the world who can put the queen's crown on your head and decide the greatest present of yours.

I meet each spring with a redoubled feeling of joy. Hardly wakened up I get up and start putting on the clothes clumsily. The happiness boiling up in my heart can hardly be explained. I celebrate for I can see the dawn and the sunny morns in July. It's a victory without a battle. Maybe it's a reward. But has the God given me the right to have the festival?! The only measures that I can use are my spiritual values. And besides, the incredible season like something that has been constant in my life excludes any possibility of pain.

When I became a student those who were in the same year as me seemed to be inextricably intertwined. It was so unusual for me. I could not call the thing by its proper name. It was unimaginable to make friends with all the people and be fond of almost everyone around me. I used to sit up in the audience and experience the feeling of estrangement. I had been trying to pick out some young people to make friends with.

My attention was drawn by a girl looking like a doll. She was so quiet and righteous. Her name is Manana. We really got on with each other. The fact that I was just a modest and reserved girl can be the only explanation of the bridge made between me and all the prosaic days.

I guess one can fall in love as many times as he finds himself to be left alone. I talk about the love between the sexes. The subconscious of a lonely one is always trying to seek for someone and that does not matter whether the search takes long or short. The heart, the thoughts, and the reason are all involved in the process. And the three marvelous virtues make it easy for one to make his love some time or other.

I did not really know him. We just had a few chats with him and nothing else. And the electricity started to move along the invisible threads in both directions. The emotion had far distanced all the feelings that I had ever experienced. I had a couple of true wings and could flutter like a being made of air. The window got larger and I could see the vault of heaven. It made me realize that any flight through the clouds takes off from the earth. And the speed of the flight proved to be so pleasant and it took too much time to touch down that the landing had to be painful enough to make me burst into tears. The beautiful dream was over and the reality was over there too. It was terrible. It was unbearable. I just separated myself from the youth having the same goals and spending their time joyfully.

The sun is even higher than one can imagine. When running up a steep path hurriedly and smiling to my favorite hill I nearly lose all the chances for the body to be saved. The walks are always exhausting for me and I have to lie down on the grass dried by the Sun. Lying on my back I can see the skies and the Sun at the same time and that's so convenient. They both look right into my face. And how very attractive the look is!!! I gather myself up and the meditation gets deeper into the cells of my brain.

Looking for the best alternative for thinking I ask the petals of an ox-eye daisy whether the man with the wide shoulders is in love with me or not. I have been working my way towards his heart. And the flower is always about one and the same. He loves me, he loves me, and he loves me. I don't know how the plant manages to make me know about the love...Please don't ask me about for the answer may sound just foolish. It's the intuition or my face all shining for I'm happy. I believe it and I smile with that greenhorn smile. I get up and look in the direction where there is the road. It's a goal, it's a light seen from the far and if you want to reach it, to melt into it, you have to pass along the way.

My alter ego that has never been afraid to be trodden upon feels knows that I need it. I've never experienced the fear too. I can feel the ego coming into me offhanded and I get as courageous as I have never been before. I think I'll be left unprotected without the second self taking care of me. I'm proud and satisfied. I want to thank my God first and the alter ego then. It will never leave me alone in the world till the end and that's the most important thing for the time is fond of different ordeals that overtake us sooner or later.

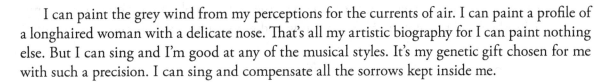

I can paint the grey wind from my perceptions for the currents of air. I can paint a profile of a longhaired woman with a delicate nose. That's all my artistic biography for I can paint nothing else. But I can sing and I'm good at any of the musical styles. It's my genetic gift chosen for me with such a precision. I can sing and compensate all the sorrows kept inside me.

When I really grew up I realized that everything taken for something necessary by the governing cells of the human brain was in conflict with the command of my heart and soul. The inner strife with the external aspects was fully presented in my disposition. The reality did not result from the dreams having a different value of happiness. In the situations like that I used to cover myself up have the inner battle for I knew that it was an optimum method to reach the peace of mind.

I loved all the characters of the books. The details of their lives had already got mine for I wanted to get through the fates. They were the only persons I could see in the reality. The heroes were my life, my weakness and the wound that had was not going to be healed. I felt pity for them. I worried about their destinies, their heavy hearts, their love and souls struggling with the treacherous reality like me.

It's obvious that in any environment that my soul is unaccustomed to it starts to rebel. I am not a time-server and it makes me enclosed in a blind alley. I cannot accommodate myself to everything and my will turns into something encroached upon. Yes, any changes and novelties make me estranged and the lack of correspondence between the soul and the body, the lability, to be more precise, makes me feel all the unpleasant feelings. It's a test to stand for or otherwise I'll have to accept everything in the world.

My mother is a wonderful woman, always calm, and thoughtful and modest. We almost never talk, though we can understand each other perfectly. She has always been the same, still, and quiet, and unoffending. The unceremonious birth of mine, her third child, was caused, I guess, just by one thing, and the thing, the reason was calling her, the extremely kind woman, my MOM!

As for my father, I avoid telling about him rather intentionally. It's painful. And I can do nothing with the pain. There's no remedy, you know. The death was so unexpected. He had been feeling ill just for three months. I hope you can understand the sorrow, the grief and my willingness to stop here. The only thing I really want to say is that there's no woe deeper than the feeling associated with the demise of someone from your family.

I got married when I saw that marriage was not somewhat of a burden. And if it really was it could never be heavier than the load of loneliness. It seemed to be much easier to shoulder it with someone else.

I'm happy for my half is a balanced and homely man and the liberty of my soul has not been curtailed since we got married. I have not changed. Full of the affection for the Sun I can still live in the dreamy clouds. Thank God!!! The only thing that has changed is that I have a daughter and a son. I have accomplished a brave feat. The sickly woman having no prospects for managing a household (we all were sure about the fact) turned out to be a perfect wife.

The girl is steady and unpretending like her father. The boy resembles almost everyone: me, my father, my brothers and my mother. He's too young and too scrupulous. You know, he's manly.

I have two brothers. They are so very different and they love so very differently. The elder one is more outspoken. He likes fondling others and telling them all the endearing words. He is an artist, a poet in his heart of hearts.

The younger brother is an unruly altruist always listening to his heart. He can do anything just out of pity for somebody or something. He can even harm himself for having compassion upon others.

My sis Dali, she's younger than me, has always been responsible for somebody. She always does her best to make others have better lives. She is more practical than me and is good in almost everything. She is a fideist.

I have always been ailing, always between life and death. The only thing that I really prayed for was my health. The relatives had always been awaiting my death. None of the years that I have passed through was remarkable for my being healthy.

And the attacks of the strange disease are still with me. I'm afraid and I take all the preventive measures. I run from a doctor to another to find it out what the disease is. My God! All the modern methods of medical examination can dot my i's and cross my t's.

And I can see the yellow paper with some German words written on it. That's the cause... The doctor in charge carrying the paper in his hands looks at me and at a colleague of his sitting nearby. They both seem to be rather astonished.

The celiac disease, one of the genetic diseases – finally uttered the man. I kept silent for good while. The name of the thing I had been suffering from told me nothing. I had never heard it. I was nervous, though I preferred not to speak. Then Goga, my doc, turned to me and told me about all the details of the illness. He said I could cope with the task and never eat bread until the death comes. Giorgi Beitrishvili, Giorgi Kvitaishvili, Tengiz Telia - these are the men whom I owe my life.

Remember, I hated bread when I was a child. It turns out now that I was right then.

Imagine a bridge swaying like a swing. There is the enormous river of Enguri running rapidly from the mounts. We want to cross the bridge. We have taken each other's hands. Our heads are swimming. It's so strange. Two sisters grip each other's palms even harder and given hope move forward. We cross it, the Rubicon of ours. We have got the symbol of the struggle with life and the thirst for human eternity.

The sky was so clear that day. I told the morn about the inoffensive desire. The idyllic and euphoric sensations are all based upon the optimism. And the happiness has nothing in common with the thing that can make us experience the flight all of a sudden and in any age. The time driving me forth to the old age at the breakneck speed is not a barrier. The age that is hardly within one's control is not a problem for me. I've never been so joyous and I feel quite well. I've never felt better. I know the anguish increasing so very silently will be changed by the great happiness for the ideas to be ruled do not require all the methods that have always been considered to be the best ones. The thoughts are easy to realize, I believe.

There can be no doubts that we all have secrets. The best defense is concealment. Though, it's artificial. There are things that cannot be stripped naked. And the aim to unravel all the hidden thoughts is not really good. If you really want to talk you have to get rid of the fear. Neither censuring nor playing the role of a true mentor can be regarded as something good. Keeping in secret things one is not eager to unveil is one thing but rummaging in souls just to ransack the souls is a sin much worse.

My Bella is a part of my flesh and a pain that I have been feeling for two months. Sitting at the bedside all gloomy I have been seeking for the consoling words to tell her... She is at the hospital now. I'm such an egoist trying not to answer her questions for the feeling of remorse will never let me say anything.

I have not touched all the important issues here. And I don't think it's good enough to be satisfied with myself. It looks like an episode, just a day from one's life that I submitted to the readers in a form that turned out to be acceptable to me. Let everyone willing compose!!! The desire to write can always be justified for any sincere word is a victory in the latent war (for me, at least) that we levy on each other right at the moment when we start breathing.

I appeared on the snow cover like edelweiss. The snow has served me as a ground to step upon that never heats me. Each morning I look for the warmth of the Light. I never draw back because of the past days full of vein expectations. And I have a boundless believe that it's the virtue of love that can raze all the pains from one's memory.

The deathless butterfly

She had already noticed the butterfly that flew through the window into the room more than once. It used to fly round the kitchen first and then sat on one of the table corners inactively with its head hung down and looking all like a pistil. Then it suddenly spread its wings and flitted about the flat smoothly. Finally it sat down on a curtain rim and stayed over there till it became dark. One and the same thing happened over and over again during those two years. She always thought that the butterflies coming in through the window were different for she knew that the life of the insects is quite short. Though, it was hard to ignore the fact that the butterfly visiting her every single day, every morning and every night never changed. Never changed the yellow specks covering it.

Lady got used to the butterfly so much that when it did not come she always went to the window, opened the curtain and waited for it. One day when she was having her breakfast the butterfly fluttered in and sat down in the corner of the table with its wings folded together like all the butterflies usually do. Lady was glad to see it. She stole up to it silently and caught it with the wings. She did not let it out of her palm for a while looking at it and willing just to caress. Finally she said to the creature:

- How beautiful you are! And your colors are so wonderful, Buttie! - She gave it the name almost unintentionally. When she let the butterfly fly out of her hand she saw that the atomic yellow spots had come off the wings almost completely and had painted her hands. The color was left only here and there. It was painful to realize that it was all because of her touch. Later on she just gazed at it and never touched it again.

It got habitual for her to have her breakfast waiting for the butterfly with expectation. She took heed to the fact that the insect was aware of the feeling and always showed up for the dinner and for the supper as well. It whirled around her head as if telling her about something. Then it sat down either in front of her or just by her side and finally twirled around the whole area.

In winter Lady decided to go to Bakuriani for a week or so. She went there every year with Zura. She had never seen the snow mantle to be as thick as it was then. She skied all day long and covered long distances like a professional skier. The time flew too quickly and she could not realize that the day of departure had already come.

A man in sportswear stopped her in the hotel lobby and started a conversation with her. The man who was much older than Lady gave her some questions about the service of the hotel with interest. She answered him politely. They talked about sports and weather then. They represented the few Georgians among too many foreigners and it made it easier for them to understand each other. They liked each other. Lady went upstairs to change her cloths.

When she entered the room she felt she was in a joyful mood for some reason. She was happy but what was it that had caused the happiness?! The man who was much older seemed to have suited her taste. She was content with something and ready to flaunt. She took a warm blue dress with long sleeves from a hanger and put it on rapidly. She spent some time in front of the mirror. Her hair was falling down to her shoulders so beautifully but the idea to pull it to the top struck her suddenly. Zura liked the hairdo. When she grasped the hair slide she discovered something that was just amazing. The butterfly with the yellow spots had found her even there. It set over there on a comb all silent. Lady cried out happily:

- Buttie, how did you find me…how lovely you are?! – She treated the creature as tenderly as she usually did. Then she turned to the hair slide. The butterfly did not stop whirling about her hands and that was the most uncommon thing about the meeting. It was not going to let her take the slide. She smiled to it and said:

- Playing with me, Buttie, move aside, I have to hurry up! - She hardly managed to take the hair slide and pinned it to her hair immediately. She looked into the glass once again, smiled to the reflection and left the room straight off without remembering her Buttie.

They sat at the restaurant till the night. His name was Misha. He was a good company. He was a man having a moderate humor and was rather well-read. They drank quite enough of champagne and told things too cheerfully…Lady who was slightly drunk did not stop to tee-hee. When he took her to the room she looked at him with the eyes of a woman in love. It was a sign for Misha that the heart of the beautiful woman belonged to him.

The next day Misha took her aback at the snowy track and asked her sweetly:

What can I do for the Snow Queen?! Please tell me.

Lady smiled to looked at him seriously:

Mr. Misha, I'm leaving for the city today!

Mister?! – He felt hurt. – Call me just Misha, right?

Right, Misha…- Lady smiled again.

Let's go tomorrow. I'm going too…

You? Why? You came here just two days ago, you said…

Why? Just because of the most important thing…the most wonderful and timely thing…- he did not finish.

OK, Mr. Misha!

That "Mister" again, - thought Misha. Maybe she addressed him so because of his age of because he was one of the President's namesakes.

Lady seemed to have guessed what his thought were about. She asked:

Who gave you the President's name?

It was my granny. The president was not born then.

How old are you Mr. Misha?

Mister… again…OK…I'll be your master starting from today

Tell me how old are you? – He could not get rid of her and her questions.

Quite old…it doesn't really matter, does it?!

Sure, Mister… - Lady looked at the sky.

I never liked all the young man…I mean those who were too young.

Really? - He was pleased.

Is there anyone looking for you in the city? – It was obvious that he was talking about her husband.

No, my lord, there's no one waiting for me, - she remembered the butterfly with the yellow specks and added, - but Buttie. And Buttie is here…

Buttie?—Misha could not understand. – Who's Buttie?

I'll make you acquainted with it. It's so strange. It lives with me.

A man or a woman? I've never heard such an odd name.

She burst into a ringing laughter so that tears bleared her eyes.

Let's see each other in the evening…Later on…Now I have to go to the hotel. – She did not tell him about the secret name. Misha leaned towards her. He touched the rose-colored face. It was neither a kiss nor a smack on the cheek. It was something different, something strange…just adoration…or something that was hard to be given any specific definition then.

Lady lied in the warm room of the hotel and thought about the butterfly. It was really strange for the insect to appear in the middle of the winter. There could be no doubt about that mysterious yarning for always being by her side… Had it accompanied her stealthily or maybe it found her only afterwards? Suddenly she jumped up to her feet. She said that she had to see Misha and opened the door. When she stepped out of the building Misha waved his hand to her from a distance. She dashed to him and asked:

Maybe you know, Misha, how many lives a butterfly can have?

Misha smiled. He wondered what had made her remember butterflies in the winter…

Butterflies…if I am not mistaken… they live just two or three days… why? What's up?

Lady became thoughtful:

No, I just asked…- She tried to smile. When they reached the stairs she said: - I have a headache, Misha! Let me take a nap. I'll see you at night, - and she walked up the stairs.

In the city Misha did his best to make her forget her Butttie; she was just driven to the point of forgetting everything else. He was too warm and caring towards the girl. She used to come home late. By the end of all the eventful days she was always tired and immediately went to bed. They had already appointed the day of the wedding party and the couple full of expectations had been looking ahead.

It was a warm day in April. Lady and Misha stood side by side at the wedding palace. She had put on a fiery dress and carried some beautiful white camellias in her hand. The hall lighted with lamps was full of guests. The wedding ritual was accompanied by some calm music. Lady looked at Misha with a warm smile and prepared the pen. She was ready to begin a new life and seemed to be happy. The first love that turned out to be so tragic had to be over too. She leaned forward and right where she had to put her signature she saw a wonderful picture…All of a sudden Buttie appeared from somewhere and started to whirl about the paper strangely so that she could not touch the sheet. She tried to make the creature fly off the place, to parry its attempts but all in vain…Then she whispered in a low voice:

Buttie, don't bother! Go, just go! - But the tiresome insect flied more and more actively as if trying to do it to spite her. It did not let her sign the paper. The best men became noisy:

What's up, what's that?!

Afraid of it? Put your signature, - said Misha, grasped the wings of the butterfly and crushed it down against the table. His indifference made her feel pain and pity for the helpless and delicate butterfly. Though, she remained impassive, affixed her signature and looked over the table where the happiest man, her bride had just pressed Buttie against the wood ruthlessly. But Buttie was alive. It was all trying to fly with its new wings. Lady was glad with the revival or raising from the dead. – Buttie! – She called the creature. She felt it was her fault. She tried to fondle it but Buttie escaped, flew up and moved towards the door. Lady followed it with her sad eyes and saw something striking that made her lose her balance…She even staggered…She hardly managed to remain of her feet.

The face of Zura Tabagari, her deceased husband was looking at her from the exit as he usually did when dressed in nice clothes she was to go somewhere alone. She came around soon. Now it was clear that the soul of the man used to come to her having assumed the aspect of the butterfly. He was always by her side and no one would ever be able to kill him.

She remembered that she had to stay in bed for some ten days in summer. She had dislocated her foot then. Buttie did not leave her. Yes, it was Zura, his bright spirit.

The expression of her face and her mood changed unexpectedly. Lady turned to Misha:

Killer! You killer! Don't touch me! - She cried out and moved backwards to the exit. Finally she hurled the camellias right in the street and ran away as fast as she could.

The fair deity

Our visits to the country always made granny Masho so very happy. She lived on the slope situated above our house. As soon as she heard us, she used to call: "Have already come"? Fussing around he did all that she could just to please us. Carrying a pail full of crispy cucumbers in one hand and a stick in another she limped down the descent. She always treated us with the cucumbers gathered in a pail. We were always glad to see her. We met her outside and peeled the plants right in the yard all sitting around the table...We peeled and peeled and ate them with a true gusto.

Granny Masho was a single woman concerning the love between a woman and a man as well as the wedlock to be something blameworthy. If one asked her why she didn't get married, she grumbled and said: "Never dare talk about again"! In such moments she always looked at the opponent angrily and tried to change the subject. To cut a long story short, she was someone maybe even unearthly whose persuasion absolutely contradicted the love relationships between the sexes.

Unfortunately her brother married a woman of easy virtue. Lia, a tall and elegant woman was quite cheerful as well. The attention of the local men was focused upon the lady who used to be always laughing and merry. She kept an open house and treated anyone met in the street with some good wine. Somehow or other all the men in the village had fallen in love with her. Her husband took no heed of the fact that seemed to be less important then. He was too credulous. He had a beautiful wife and whether willing or unwilling he tried to avoid all the suspicions and problems.

Masho often caught her brother alone and hurled reproaches at him because of his spouse's behavior. He always listened carelessly and left the woman without uttering a word. It was a true reason for the damnation of Masho who spent days spying upon her sister-in-law. She had to know where the woman went, who the people that she talked to was and what was the thing that they were about. It was a permanent watch to catch the woman napping.

Lia, full of joie de vivre, wanted to find some boundless love, though her husband appeared to be inattentive towards the woman. He had just no backbone and that was all. There was nothing strange in her quest for the true feelings. First she had an adventure with the chairman of the collective farm. They had a child together. The tractor driver called Vano happened to be the next and she gave birth to a curly-headed little boy. Neither the club manager nor the stock-farm director did bear her a grudge too. She had six children and it was not a secret for anyone in the village that only the eldest, Tekle was Carlo's daughter.

Lia's brother had left the country for Russia for already 12 years. That summer he managed to come back and lived alone in the house that had been deserted since the time their parents died. From time to time the neighbors came and told some stories of what had been going on in their village. He listened to them attentively for he had missed the lifestyle.

Granny Masho decided to tell about his sister to the man. One morning she took her stick that was almost inseparable, put on a headscarf and doddered to Besso's place. She sat down in the yard and told the brother all the details about his sister with a puzzled look. She promised to catch Lia and her lover red-handed and do whatever one had to do then.

Poor Besso got just furious. In the mountainous part of the land it was something just inadmissible, intolerable. Unfaithfulness of a woman has always been regarded there as an affront to the dignity of her husband, her brother and the whole kin. It was not a thing for Besso that could be easily forgotten. He could hardly believe that his own sister had dragged their name through the mud. No, no, it was too terrible to be real. Even when he was a boy he knew that Masho was fond of making up. "Maybe it's another delusion, another lie", - thought the man and started to walk up and down the yard. The emotions made him drink a whole bottle of vodka later and he fell asleep rested against the fence.

Self-satisfied Masho came home knocking the stick down of the ground right when her sister-in-law was setting the table. Masho refused to sit down with a frown when Lia politely asked her to dine with them. She looked around angrily and went out to the cornfield.

Besso drank more and more frequently. He drank day after day. The countrymen really felt pity for him. One evening the youth decided to go to the club to see some film and we were among them. We ran into heavily drunk Besso lying on his back right on the grass. We felt sorry for him and decided to call Aunt Lia for he was absolutely alone and unprotected. We first went up the path leading to granny Masho's house but having been in a hurry to get to the club in time we preferred the short cut and went through the cornfields. All of a sudden I stumbled over something and twisted my foot. I screamed out for it was painful. The children came to help me asking what was up. Though, the only thing that I could realize then was that I was lying on somebody's body and I could not get up.

It lasted quite long. Some bodies were moving just under my own one, though I could see nothing because of the darkness. I even heard some whispering voices there. I trembled with fear. The ache in my leg made me call the children for help and cry out: "Don't touch me"! We had almost reached granny Masho's house. They left me in the cornfield and Nelly ran up the slope that we called aunt Lia's slope and started to shout in a loud voice. "What are you galloping around for"? – asked granny Masho. Her lamp lit the field and we could see one another pretty well. The woman started to utter some shrill scream. "Lia! Vano! Lia! Vano"! – cried out Masho madly. We could all see how the tractorist and Aunt Lia, Masho's sister-in-law were running away pushing away the ear stems. With my foot still aching I stood over there leaning against a pear tree and looked with an inquiring look first at granny Masho and then at the couple who had already got quite far.

A few months passed. However, people did not stop talking about the fact. Things like that were uncommon there. Mediators came to their families every single week. Though, it turned out to be impossible to reconcile them. Finally it was decided to appear before the Deity.

It was a cold day in November. Some men had already gathered at the church built at the highest point of the mountainous village. Some of them stood with their eyebrows frowned together in front of the shrine looking down into the earth. They were all silent. Lia's brother, her husband and cousins stood together, on the opposite side there were Vano and his family. According to the Svanetian customs, the ritual had to be held at St. George's church after two months from the event. Vano and his people were to swear they were innocent and the woman and the man had never had a conversation. If they swore they would make it up with each other. But if they lied, all the men in their family would die. In short, the strange rite had to be administered in line with the existing traditions and that was the reason of the gathering.

Vano and his relatives swore that the man had never had a conversation with Lia. With one accord swore the brothers. The Svanetian rules obliged the sides to reconcile, though the noise did not stop then. People anticipated something terrible for they knew for sure that no liar could ever rid himself of an ill fate. "What are they going to do? They lied before the Deity and they'll be punished"!- were the words that one could hear hither and thither.

Vano had a dream that night: he saw his very old grandpa sitting on the leader's seat. His impression was just exacting. Waving the stick in a weird manner the man started to move towards his grand-son. He also had some other thing in his hand. Though, Vano failed to remember what exactly the thing was, he thought it would be the icon of St. George. Suddenly the old man became uproarious. "You, you scoundrel, you have brought shame upon your family" – shouted the man. "What shall I tell your father"? Vano, who had lowered his gaze could not look into grandfather's face. He was ashamed. "You will all come here soon and I'll show you then", - said the ghost and disappeared. When the tractor driver woke up he had no doubts left about the ill fate that was close enough and he knew that the others were going to share the destiny with him.

In the most beautiful part of the world there is river flowing all in foam and all in a hurry. It often brings down some giant clods and trees tore out of the earth with their roots. It's the River of Inguri. It has already taken up many, many lives without mercy.

On the bank of the river there were parts of a knocked-down car scattered all over. Last night both brothers disappeared into the water that had enormously risen and was rolling along rhyming its own rhymes. Voices of an yelling women could be heard from the other end of the village. Everyone had come to the bank. They all stood there with their heads hung down and sad, wistful faces. Each person who had come to the place knew that it was the Deity and its revenge.

Granny Masho was among them. She spoke in a strict voice again, though the sounds had turned weaker than usual. She was crying. "Look at the misfortune, people! It's the Deity taking vengeance on the family"! Then she started to cry out the words of sorrow even louder and said: "That was not the thing I've been seeking for, that was not the thing"… The echo of the mounts faintly imitated her wailing.

In spring his horse threw off one of Lia's sons into a ravine. The boy died there. He was the child that Lia and Vano had together. People knew it and talked about the father who lied and his son who was punished for the guile.

In the distinguished part of our country each word has some special and magic strength. If one breaks his word he has almost nothing left to hope for. Though, others who are always as good as their words are just blessed. It has been a rule since the ancient times and nothing will ever change until the Earth and the Heaven, the part of the World and the Svanetians living there don't stop their lives.

The horse in the secret

He had a white horse. It was white like one made of snow. It had dark and sad eyes. One might have thought that the horse could understand every single word exactly. It looked at you until you told him a whole story. If you stopped the horse used to hang its head down and was always hot to trot looking into the earth. He seemed to be begging: - please, go on! He had an inquiring stare and could wag its tail in response. Sometime he made a nervous noise with his heels. In any event it was not a problem to guess what the horse was about.

When the brothers divided their property the horse was the only thing that had fallen to Givi's lot. They were too needy. Givi was content with the lot. He took the bridle and began to construct a house on a barren knoll. He brought some stones from the river with the horse and gathered them on the hill. Soon his house was the best one in the part of the world.

He had too many friends, relatives and neighbors, but the horse was the closest one among them. Bero was the name of the beast. Yes, it was the most faithful and staunch Bero. No one could understand him better than the horse that always managed to calm him down with that snorting. When he was glad Bero always met the man neighing. It was the only witness when he stepped out stealthily. When he was in disagreement with somebody the horse used to be his confidant. The sympathy felt by the horse could never be compared with the compassion expressed by the men.

One day an old acquaintance of his came to Givi's place. He was glad to see the guest. Willing to treat the man in an appropriate manner he put some bread and wine on the table. They drank too much and finally went out. Suddenly Zakro saw the horse. He was enraptured and said:

-What a nice horse you have, Givi! I don't think there can be a horse like this one not only in the region but even throughout the world. – The words flattered Givi. He answered: - last year a foreign traveler offered me a good sum for it. Thank God he was a foreigner…Yes, I'd show him…- he shook his head with a threatening countenance. It was clear for Zakro that Givi cherished the horse as an apple of his eye…A shiver went up and down his spine.

When Givi got twenty years old his father brought him to the center to buy a horse. They had been willing to buy one for quite long. There were too many customers gathered at Lazare's house. Zakro and his brother had come too. The owner wavered. He did not worry about money he just wanted to find a good patron for the horse. Finally he walked slowly towards the crowd, came to Givi and said for everybody to hear: - A good horse needs a good rider! – And he handed the bridle to the boy. Givi thanked him joyfully, patted the horse's mane, bridled the beast and mounted it swiftly…His father paid for the horse and called Givi: - Go home, son! I have to set some things going. I'll be back soon. - Then he turned to the disappointed customers, gave a nod of politeness and went away.

Zakro gnashed his teeth with anger. First he thought to make Givi turn back and beat him black and blue together with his brother. But it was not easy to beat the boy. He decided to allay his anger and went home.

Givi called the horse, touched its mane again and said:

He's our guest, let him ride, show him the lanes and come home in peace. – Zakro walked round the stallion. Bero wagged its tail angrily. It was a surprise for Givi but in spite of that he thought he was the only one that the horse really loved. – He even smiled with pleasure and said to Zakro: - You can take it. – Zakro glad with the suggestion put the saddle on the steed, got on its back quickly and flew away from the place. He rode too far and disappeared from the view together with the horse. Givi looked at them for a while and said hopefully: - They'll be back. – Then he lied down. He slept till the evening. When he woke up he looked for the horse and the guest. He sought for them hither and thither. Though, he failed to find them. He became thoughtful…Impossible…Where could they have gone…There was no reason in thinking about a peril. The horse was even clever than some people.

Two days later Bero came home. It was exhausted and splashed with mud. He had some blood traces left on the body. Givi examined the horse. He appeared many abrasions and wounds. He had no bridle. Givi was alarmed and started to question the animal.

What happened? Where have you been? Why didn't you come home and where's Zakro? – asked Givi. The horse looked to the east and began to sniff. It was not a good sign. The horse was gloomy. Givi fell to thinking.

- Take me to the place you're coming from, - said Givi to the horse and got on it. The beast ran away so that Givi hardly managed to control his body. Eventually they reached a chasm. Bero ruffled up its mane - another bad sign. The two had their own language. He got down from the horse and approached the abyss. There was a vast gulf lying before him. He experienced a sudden horror. Did he fall down into the deeps?- Zakro he cried down at the top of his voice.

The mounts returned the echo.

In the terrible silence one could hear some noise reminding a voice of an animal rather than a human one. Givi looked up at Bero. He said something to the horse and the horse neighed in reply. Givi began to get down the precipice…He rolled down first. If there had not been a root of a tree, he would have disappeared completely. He crawled and crawled down, too far that he really passed out of sight. The horse neighed and hoofed against the ground as if trying to console the man.

Later the horse got anxious and started to run back and forth. Then it came to the steep and made some strange sounds. Givi was creeping up the slope together with Zakro tied to his belt. Zakro was more dead than alive. The steed neighed again and wagged the tail towards them. Givi winded the horse-hair round his hand and Bero pulled them out easily. They stopped at a safe place. Givi put his arms round the horse's neck. - My dear! - uttered the tired man and even lost his consciousness for a minute or so. He was too weary.

Zakro could hardly breathe. He had spent two days in the abyss. Givi just hung him over the saddle, fixed his head with his own hands and they got under way.

The village was situated far away from the place. They only just reached the house. The local doc lived in the vicinity. Givi opened a table drawer, wrote a letter hurriedly and fastened it to the horse's neck. - Bero, go, go to Lado! - The beast knew where he had to go to. It moved towards the doc's house. At the threshold it began to sniff and kick the hoofs against the ground. Lado rushed out immediately. He saw Bero, Givi's horse impatiently making noise with its heels. He was surprised at the sight when he noticed the note at the neck of the beast. He took the paper off, read the message and looked at the animal lovingly: - you're much better than many of us! - He said tenderly and followed the horse immediately.

They saved Zakro's life. Lado came to see him every single day. He dressed the wound again and again, and gave him some pieces of good advice. As for Zakro, his behavior was too strange. He did not answer the questions. Zakro kept silent with his head always hung down. One day when the doc sent Givi to the drugstore, Zakro started to speak: - I wanna tell you something, Lado! I'm a shameless villain, I know. You have to listen to me...my heart is going to break...- suddenly he stopped. The hush lasted for quite long. Finally Lado made up his mind to talk again: - tell me, I'm all ears...

"What a brazen man I am...I don't even know how to begin". - He took a rest, just got time to catch his breath and went on. "To tell you the truth, I hated all the people, especially those who used to be my rivals. I wanted to always be the first one. And I turned out to be the worst kind of man in the things that have always been the most important. The horse happened to be a man better than me. It's capable of loving. It was the horse who made me open my eyes to the truth. Now I know all about my wretched heart".

"I hated Givi and his horse. Me and my brother, we were both to buy the foal from Lazare. But he decided to give it to Givi for some reason. And I had been experiencing the hatred towards them since the time, for years, you know. I wanted to kill them, the horse and the owner. I could do nothing with the blood lust. I came to his place purposely, drank and made him drink on purpose too. Then I decided to take the upper road. I wanted to have done with the horse first and then with Givi. I sought for the abyss beforehand to knock the horse over it. Then I was going to do the same with Givi".

Zakro could hardly breathe. Lado passed some water to him, - have it, -he said. – Zakro took a gulp and continued: "We fought much. The horse that had pranced was badly trying to defend himself. I beat him on the hind legs to force him eventually down into the chasm. He seemed to be begging to leave him alone. I beat and beat to bring him down. I drew blood. All the attempts of the beast to stop me were vain. I fell down into the abyss instead of the horse. He desperately tried to pull me out but I had tired it down. If the horse had not been so clever and Givi had not been so brave the ravens would have eaten me up over there. It's too painful to realize that the horse knows what I was about then. I was trying to kill me. He is more generous than me. Aware of everything he wanted to rescue me. I am not the man to be saved, doc! There was no need to do it for me"! – Zakro spoke breathlessly and cried.

At the very moment Givi brought some drugs into the room, put them on the table and went out. The horse was browsing at the spring. Givi ran to the beast like a little boy and said:

Zakro is saved, Bero! – He smiled at the stallion joyfully and kissed him on the nose. The horse answered with a neigh.

- And still what happened then, Bero? - Givi often asked the horse that time on. Bero looked at his patron with the feeling of love in his eyes and kept silent. He did not want to give away Zakro's secret. He worried about Givi and knew for sure that the man would never forgive the turncoat who'd come to his place disguised as a well-wisher.

The king of boulevard

He had been called the King of boulevard since the time he began to walk along the lane in front of his house. He sits over there for hours till the night comes even if there's nobody over there. The whole point is that there's no place in the world where he has to hurry to. He is a twenty-years- old single and finds himself at ease at the place as nowhere else on the earth. He can see the views of the city, all the streets lit with lampions and glittering houses from the place and goes tome at half past twelve just because he remembers that one has to go to bed. He'll stay at work for a while the next day.

Young ladies are very much fond of touch-me-not Gegi. They smile to him from a distance. They are always anxious to take a glance of the rather handsome boy. Many of them have been trying to get acquainted with him but he always takes his time over. He watches them posing and pretends to be blind to the showing off.

Sometimes he disappears for months. There's no doubt that the girls never miss the disappearance and seek for him everywhere in the street, in the subway and in shops. Maybe he has gone out of the city. And there's no light burning in the windows of his apartment.

There lived two persons in the flat. They differed too much. Their spiritual and everyday lives had nothing in common. One of them was too cold and ambitious. And the other one was kind and amicable. In the everyday life his state peeped out through his actions…always differing… felt by the hearts of two persons and seen by the eyes of the couple.

He had inherited a business in the city. He owned a confectionary. Though, he knew nothing about the business and had trusted it to a friend of his father's who had never left him. He shared the income with the man and had such reliance upon him. He just called at the factory in the morning and entered into conversation with the workers just only if he was drunk. By the end of each month he used to get a handsome salary. Then dressed in his black or blue suit he left for somewhere (maybe for Europe) for about two or three weeks.

There was a nice man inside him exactly when he was at the back of beyond. He drank periodically and his temper changed obviously in the very periods. The frank and joyful man turned into an impressionable one.

The age had made him even more handsome. His hair was now touched with grey and his smile got even more sincere. When he was drunken he wanted to marry someone. It was his heart looking for some love. Though, it was quite another story when he grew sober. He never thought of marriage and kept himself as far as possible from the girls.

Once he was drunk and strolled along the boulevard. He saw a girl away from him. She was walking over a dog. She passed along the long path without noticing him. She sat down on the edge of the bench standing at the end of her route. Now Gegi examined her closely. He looked into her face so admiringly and so warmly that the girl was just astonished. She turned to the poodle she was keeping on a leash. The dog was as snowy as his owner. Gegi liked the girl too much and thought that it was her whom he had been seeking for. He decided not to kick about and came to the girl.

What's his name? –he asked respectfully.

She was a foreigner and could not understand what the boy was about. She made a gesture meaning that she failed to understand him. They both smiled. The gesture together with the laughter made them closer in some way. Gegi did not know what to say and there was no reason in speaking. He tried to talk in the sign language. He had studied dactylology quite well for his neighbor on the floor was a deaf-and-dumb boy. And they were of the same age. When all the deaf-mute came to his place they used to talk on the balcony so that Gegi had an opportunity to observe how the people managed to tell one another the long stories with their fingers. He wanted to learn the language and bought a special book. Soon he could serve you as a football observer, teach you a lesson of Geography or history inapproachably with all the wars and developments in the language.

And the dactylology studies just to satisfy his curiosity came in handy to him. He moved the long and dainty fingers in a manner that the girls could not tear her eyes off him. She knew nothing about the sign language and thought that the man had taken for a dumb. Then she took a German passport from her bag, brought it right to his eyes and smiled to him so sweetly that he flushed. The snow-white face, dark blue eyes, long straw-colored hair and thick lips looking as ones of an offended person made the lady-killer go off his head. The desire to fondle her was so strong that he put his arms round the dog's neck, looked into its eyes lovingly and kissed it on the nose. Mickey was so pleased with the dandling that jumped up to the man's knees and held its breath. The girl started to laugh with a ringing laughter.

Suddenly she looked down at her watch. She seemed to be in a hurry. When she got up Gegi made a sign with his hands that he was going to take her through the boulevard. She did not refuse to be accompanied by him. They stopped at a bus station near the road ending. Gegi was trying to tell her something with his fingers. I guess he was asking her to go out on a date with him. Though, she looked at him in a wide-eyed astonishment and was shaking her head declining the invitation. He could not understand what the reason of the refusal was and peered into her face with his eyes full of all the questions.

Meanwhile the bus arrived and she started to get ready to go. Gegi looked at the number of the vehicle unintentionally. It was number 20 moving along the central street. Maybe she lives in the hotel "Sakartvelo", - he thought. Before he had time to say something with his fingers again the girl grasped the dog and got on the bus. She looked at him just once and waved her hand to him. He was completely stunned. He did not know where to go to find her. He had neither the address nor anything else. He started to rush about. He was almost on his guard... He had neither her address nor a single point from her. Then he ran after the bus as if he had remembered something. He ran after it to the first stop, then to the second one...He almost caught it up but when there was just a step left to the stopped bus it started off at full speed leaving a considerable distance between the disappointed man and itself.

The boy from the dreams of many girls runs after the bus all puffing out. He takes a rest for a while and goes on running again. He runs as fast as he can... oops, the door... he gets on it. Gegi sighed with relief and looked round. There was no girl in the bus. She had disappeared without leaving a trace. The passengers looked at him suspiciously. Gegi hung his head down and alighted from the bus. When he looked at the front side of the vehicle he saw the large figures indicating the number 617.

No one had seen him in the boulevard since the day for quite long. He started to attend some courses of German and spent his time in studying the language. He happened to be right about the hotel "Sakartve" and the German girl living in it. Susan, it was her name. He used to send a note and a huge, nice bouquet to her. A man from the hotel helped him. He did his best to study German. He was looking for the moment when he would happen to be successful enough to make her agree to have a rendezvous with him.

He was surprised himself for he was successful enough to combine drinking and studying. There was a dictionary of German language lying before her. She wrote some words from the open book into an exercise-book. They drank some natural "Chacha" vodka brought from the Kakheti region...

The girls who often sauntered in the boulevard sought for him in vain. Finally they said good-bye to all the hopes. It was clear for them that the king of boulevard had been busy and was not going to have a walk again over there.

One day Gegi came to the hotel as he usually did. There was a piece of unexpected news waiting for him. It was a shock. He stood in the hotel lobby together with the receptionist. They had a heated discussion. The expression of his face could easily make one think that someone had cheated him bitterly. A month ago the receptionist told him something about the girl that later appeared to be wrong. She said the girl was not going to leave for a while and she had already gone when he came that morning. Now he has a note written by her in his hand. – Thank you for the flowers. I'm leaving for my country where the count has been waiting for me. I want Mickey to stay with you. - He looked at the paper thoughtfully quite long. You might have thought he had to solve a difficult problem. One of the hotel workers approached him with slow steps. He had a leash of the puddle in one hand. The dog seemed to have recognized Gegi; it leaped up and looked at him. Gegi leaned forward, took the dog in his hands, put it against his breast warmly went out of the hotel.

And the favorite of the ladies came back to the boulevard. With the white poodle in his hands he had a walk every single day. When he saw the admirers who had already got married, he looked at them with a feeling of shame. He loved the foreigner so much and was not going to get married at all.

Once he came to his senses and the cold face and the indifferent nature were back too. He said: Thank God! Susan has gone and I have to turn the dog out of the house. Micky did not want to go and used to return always when the man pushed him out. Finally Gegi took the dog to the most out-of-the-way part of the city and tied him to an electricity pole. It was winter time. He hurried up to his house and the snow was hitting him on the face because of the wind. He could hear the whimpering sounds of the dog from behind. Mickey was begging just not to leave him alone but what could he do with the hard heart.

A week later Mickey came home. When the dog saw the familiar door he was too glad and started to scratch the door. That night Gegi had fallen asleep tipsy drunk. He did not hear anything. In the morning he swallowed some vodka again, got ready to go out and opened the door. He saw a dead poodle at the wall. The dog had put his head against the door poorly and died. Gegi grabbed the dog and tears ran out of his eyes. Those were the tears of pity. - I'm sorry Mickey! Forgive me, please!!! - whispered the man and hugged the beast tight. He could do nothing with the tears in the street. The people passing by followed him with their eyes. Suddenly he stopped as if an idea had occurred into his mind. He walked up the stairs with the dog in his hands.

At midnight he went out of the house silently. He was carrying a spade and a bundle. He moved towards the boulevard. Chose a place, stopped over there and began digging. He buried the small, white poodle and sat down on a bench. He was sad and doleful.

It was snowing but the cold did no matter for him for he had been feeling the deep sorrow. The only thing that he realized was that there were two persons living inside him: the callous and kind man sat over there with the worn out expression of his face. And he hated the unfeeling man gotten into him so much that he was eager to give him up together with the dog.

The last will

The old man came slowly to the spring, sat down and put a pitcher under the water welling up from the earth. The round-shouldered man was about seventy-eight years old. The pain in the small of his back made it hard for him to walk. There was no one in the village to talk with him. The desire to have a company sometimes made him speak to his own shadow. -It's a man too, - he said and used to share all that had hoarded up in his heart with it. That was somewhat of a cure not to have his heart broken. He had not seen his children for ages. And the five families had moved to somewhere else. He was left all alone in the village with six households in it. Was it a village at all?

He had three children. Two of them lived abroad and the third one was in Tbilisi. He could not even remember when the latter saw him. He came by car with his friends then, said just a few words, took some twenty liters of whine from the cellar and got back into the car again.

I have to go, dad! – He said in a hurry and let the old man who looked at the leaving man until he was hidden from the view. Then he wiped his eyes and said something to himself or rather to the shadow standing by his side.

If his wife was alive there would be no problem for the man with the bad children. Martha would have helped him to overcome all the troubles. – But who are they like the mongrels…He put his hand against his heart and sighed out. Who on earth is going to inter me…- he said to his own silhouette again and staggered into the house…

His children and their families made up twelve persons, his own flesh and blood. He did not even know some of them. Yes, the old man…who will ever need the exhausted and decrepit old man, Grandpa Dito. They lead their untroubled lives. Thank God! He had the pension, though it was not enough he could buy something at least: medicines, provisions and even a warm winter jacket.

On Sunday he decided to go to the neighboring village where the country fairs used to be held. There was a chemist's shop there too. He bought his pain-killer at the shop. He had not bought it for quite long and the pain had got even sharper. I'd rather have my children with me said the man to the shadow that accompanied him now from the left and now from the right. He was too overwhelmed by grief and disappointment.

He took a rest several times before he reached the village. Some of the people gathered there recognized Granny Dito while others failed. They of them asked after his children living in the city and in Europe. Dito only heaved a sigh and gave no answer. – Maybe you know someone homeless? – he asked. He was much used to talking with the silhouette and considered it to be difficult to talk with men. He always kept his eyes looking down into the earth. He stopped at the nearest vault and looked round the people over there.

At the door of the Chemist's shop he caught a glance of his wife's cousin. He turned round at once unwilling to be noticed. They all were about one and the same thing: his children. He was filled with a deep shame at their being so indifferent. He thought it was his fault that they did not feel love towards him. They seemed not to have ever missed their father.

Granny, granny! – A little boy with a rabbit in his hand asked him to keep the small beast for him for a while. He put the white rabbit into the man's hands and ran away. – Where are you going to, boy? – Dito hardly managed to say the words when he saw the boy running down a slope. It was almost impossible to catch sight of the running kid. Granny Dito looked at the threatened beast with pity, patted its head and started to think about something. - Who was it? Where was he running to? It's all the same, I have to wait for him, – he whispered to the shadow of his own and sat down on a tree block.

A few minutes passed. Though, there was no sign of the boy. Dito looked in the direction of the slope with his eyes full of expectation. Just a jiffy ago the boy ran down the descent like mad. - What can I do with the rabbit? How long am I going to sit waiting for him? - He could not realize what was going on and sat on the block with the white beast squeezed in his hands.

Pending his return the old man murmured again: - No, I have to wait! - He drank some water from his travelling glass, patted the hair of the white rabbit tenderly and looked at the slope over again. All of a sudden a man dressed in a long cloak dashed to him crying. He swore: - Look, I found the filchers! I've got you! Where's the robber, where's your grandson? – The man kept on shouting and abusing. Then he rushed to the old man, snatched the rabbit out of his hands and pushed him down. – Take that, and take that! – said the man and went away. Granny Dito could not get up. His hat had fallen down from his head. He was trying to grasp at the earth. Some people ran to him and helped him to stand up. They asked why the man had beaten him. Dito did not answer. He just puffed out and dragged himself along the road. – Oh, how unjust the life is! – Said the man to the silhouette and continued his way home.

He walked quite long. When he stopped at the spring to have a rest he smiled bitterly. When he was young he used to run up the hill in a twinkling of an eye. Yes, that's the old age! - He emitted a moan and stood up sluggishly. - Grandpa, grandpa! – Dito started. He shadowed his eyes with his hand and looked in the direction from where he could hear the voice. – Who can it be? – thought the man and went to the stranger joyfully.

The boy was approaching him slowly. He was about ten or eleven years old. When he came nearer the old man recognized him. The boy stood before him shyly and hardly managed to utter:

Granny, I'm sorry! Please... I didn't want to…They hurt you because of me! Sorry, grandpa! Sorry – The boy shed bitter tears and Dito's heart filled with sympathy.

Come near, sonny! That's all right, that's all right! Calm down, dear! – He caressed the boy like a grandchild of his own and held him tight. He stood there embraced with the boy trying to experience the affinity that one can feel with respect to his grandchildren. Then he asked the boy:

Where do you live, son! What's your name? - The boy who seemed to be ashamed said in a low voice:

Beqa, that's my name. I'm a waif. I can sleep anywhere. Last night I slept in the corridor of the school in Dzegvi. Sometimes I sleep on the balcony of the chemist's shop. I stole the rabbit from the man for I want to breed some rabbits. If I had a hundred of the beasts I would buy uncle Rostoma's house in Avchala…Then I'll breed them again and buy some clothes, and a telephone to call my friend in Sukhumi. He remained there and I want to know whether he is alive or not…

What about your parent's, son? – Tears were sparkling in Dito's eyes.

No, during the war all the people were trying to leave Sukhumi. Dad seated me in uncle Shakro's Kamaz truck and sent me to Tbilisi. They said that the Russin killed my parents that day.

Granny Dito put his arms round the boy. He was shivering all over. Beqa turned to him:

Why are you shivering granny! Are you cold?

Take me home, Beqa! Will you do it for me, sonny?

I'll do…

I live in the house standing on the slope…Will you stay with me? - said Granny Dito with a trembling voice.

I'll stay, granny! Thank you! – They stood there for a while. Dito hardly breathed. He felt such a pity for the poor Boy.

Let's go, son…- he grasped his hand and they both walked up the rise.

The old man had a rest once and then went on again. Beqa accompanied him with the travelling glass in one hand and Granny Dito's horny hand in another.

In spring Dito had already had a cornfield, vineyard and some rabbit-hutches behind the house. He had spent his insignificant pension to fulfill the wish of the boy. He bought two rabbits first, then three and four and had already bred them. Beqa was always busy working in the household. He had brought too much joy to the place. The happiness had turned Granny Dito into a cheerful and active man.

In autumn Beqa got fifteen. Early in the morning Granny Dito took some rabbits to the city, sold them there and bought a mobile phone for the boy. He was glad to have the wish of the orphan granted. He walked up the slope as if he had not been suffering from the pain in his knees for ten years. Only when he sat down in the yard his heart started to beat so strongly and he breathed too heavily that one might have thought that the organ propelling his blood was going to rupture. Beqa ran to bring some medicine. When he was all right again he asked the boy to come nearer and took the present out of his pocket.

- Take it sonny! Call him! Call him in Sukhumi and tell your friend he can come to our place any time! – He said jerkily.

Beqa could not get a wink of sleep that night. He found out that his friend Gela had moved to Tbilisi. The neighbors told him the boy's address too. He could not let the phone out of his hand. Granny Dito had never slept so well. We woke up earlier than usual and sat down in the yard by Beqa.

Dear, if I die bury me over there! - He pointed to the cemetery. - You are the patron of everything here! The testament is in the last drawer of the chest. No one will ever contend for the things even if they were made of gold…- he added sorrowfully.

Beqa did not respond. He salted a corncob and gave it to Granny.

No, son, have you forgotten? My teeth, I don't have...- he smiled to the boy and got up.

Granny Dito closed the door of the cellar and started to hum some old melody

When Dito died it appeared that there had been only one man who had never left him. Beqa paid homage to the old man. He went to the cemetery every single day and talked with the deceased as if he was still alive:

Granny, two more rabbits were born today.

Granny, I have hoed the cornfield.

Granny, I gave my son your name.

Granny, no one has come from the city, - he used to say in the end sadly for he knew it for sure that it had been the most important thing for Granny Dito. Yes, he knew that Granny had been waiting for his children till the very last minutes of his life.

The laughter in the War

There used to walk a sullen man along that street. His expression could easily make you think that someone had just wounded his feelings. Everyone there took him for one of a somber character. Even his greetings used to be so rude and harsh that people asked one another: - What's up with him? What's eating him? No one had ever seen him smiling. It was hard to understand what pleased or harmed him. To cut a long story short, he was an odd man.

- It's because of his age. Was he just the same in his youth? – He had given rise to a lot of talk. Though, he was young enough, say, fifty years old. People tried to talk to him warmly but nothing came out of the attempts. Rezo had been looking neither for their warmth nor the caress. The angry neighbors were fed up with all the staff and started to malign against him:

Maybe he has run mad or maybe it's his climacteric.

There was a Georgian bakery on the street and the peculiar man lived on its opposite side. He had a good house and a good job. He had a family: smiling children a wife just as gloomy as himself.

It was a riddle for the neighbors how the couple managed to have the brisk and friendly offsprings.

The flavor coming out of the bakery could be felt throughout the street. The bakers were always busy baking for the people stood in long, long lines. Once the baker y was set on fire. The sparkling fire forced the dwellers run out of their homes. Before they called in a fire engine the man who had always been scowling and pouting crawled up to the roof the of the baker house, brought a rubber hose through his window and when the fire-fighting vehicle turned at the corner of the street the fire had been almost extinguished. The devotion caused another wave of rumors among the neighbors.

How brave he is, how selfless! He even risked his life…

He was a surgeon. During the war he went to Tskhinvali as a volunteer. His wife said nothing then. She just shrugged her shoulders meaning that it was up to him. He put his instruments in a large bag, packed up his belongings and went away. It was another shock for the people around him.

– He left the family…paid no attention to his age…He is so strange, - they talked.

Now his wife went to work even more angrily. She passed by the people she met just like a foe. She'd never answer you even if you called her. That's why the kids of the street hidden at the front door often called her: Aunt Nato! Aunt Nato! – They dared do it for they knew she would never have turned.

Their children had been waiting for the war to be over. They watched all the TV programs attentively. Waiting for the head of the family they used to stand outside. Though, he wasn't going to appear. Three months of expectation passed. He had already been there for three years but they knew nothing about him. All the doubts about his death seemed to have some real ground.

Lado and Lali got married. Lado named his son for his father. He was proud of the decision and walked with his little Rezo in the street in a really dignified manner. He was as cheerful as he used to be in his childhood. But the boy kept his eyebrows always frowned together. The child was the exact image of his grandpa always scowling and pouting. Even all the clowns in the world with all their tricks wound have failed to make him smile.

Very often Nato put a heavy bag on her back and went somewhere with a businesslike gait. No one knew where she was going to. It was her own business and it was a secret. Once some people saw her at the Patrol Force. She had filed too many complaints charging almost everyone in Rezo's disappearance. The President, the police and the whole world....they were all blamed.

A heavy shower started one morning. It was followed by the flakes of the early snow. Rezo who had just got off a bus had got soaked to the skin. It did no matter to him. He was so glad to be back home that stepped right into the huge puddles. He was happy to see the city again. He looked in wide-eyed astonishment at the street that had changed too much. Where is my family? Maybe they have moved, - he thought. When he came into the porch he burst into laughter. There was really nothing to laugh at, but he was just happy. He went up the stairs to the second floor of the house. Three years ago he walked down the stairs in a gloomy mood and no one would even dare ask him where he was going to. It was a strange state of happiness. He met his neighbor living on the same floor. The man did not recognize him...He had never seen Rezo smiling.

Rezo felt hurt for the neighbor seemed to be cold towards him. – Hello, Vasso! – He called after him. Vasso looked at him in a constrained manner, just nodded and went on.

It was his wife who opened the door. – I've missed you so much, - he took the woman into his arms. His eyes were sparkling with excitement. She ran out. - It's me, Nato, it's Rezo... Nato couldn't hear the words for she had already gone far.

Then we went to his children. They were glad to see him but they failed to smile as they usually did for his joyfulness was somewhat of a strange. – What's up with him, - was the only thing that they could think about.

Nato didn't even let him get nearer. He had to go out and burst out the enormous energy. It was a way for him to let everything out of his heart. In the street he greeted the people he knew and told them some anecdotes. As for the strangers, he told them the stories of the war with humor.

He knew no tiredness in the war where he had to look after the wounded. He had been considered to be unobliging there too before it happened. There were too many wounded men that he had to take care of. One of them was shot right in his belly. The man had already bled profusely and his heart had stopped beating. Rezo knew that it was impossible to revivify the dead man but he did what he had to do and cleared his abdominal cavity. He did everything that he was used to do during all the ordinary operations. All the procedures were over and the tired surgeon washed his hands. When he sat down he felt some strange warm puffing. It was his soldier breathing. He put his stethoscope against the breast of the wounded man and when he had no doubts about the revival he almost roared with laughter. He had never laughed so…The soldier was saved and Rezo has been always in good temper since the day. When the war was over he asked the soldiers to bring some wine. He drank much and made others drink with him. God knows which time he proposed a toast to the life telling others what a precious gift it was.

I'll tell you, it's good to live, to war, to be alive! – Then he drank and started to sing. The hardship and the war have taught him how he was to laugh and he laughed with that loud and resounding laughter. A week later he followed the soldier to his country as an attending medical doctor. He seemed to haveforotten about the family waiting for him.

Now it was not easy to stop the man who had never laughed. He laughed right in the street and even bothered the people living there with the needless joy.

- It's boring, - they though and got back to the rumors.

Nato did not admit him to her life. She loved that sullen Rezo who never smiled and always kept his eyebrows together. She had nothing to do with the joyful one and spent the rest of her life in looking for the gloomy, gloomy, gloomy man.

The loonys royalties

The woman and her son used to be the first ones to wake up in the court. Though, no one can awaken if he never sleeps. They had been sleepless for years always keeping vigil. They had definitively mixed the daytime with the night...It was a story of a restive lifestyle and, to be more precise, of reckless minds. They were unable to apprehend things as they were. The woman who was not less sick than her insane son was always treading on his heels:

Have it...sit down over there...keep silent...take the pill... - Five times a month their neighbors called the service officers for the man driven mad with all the advices of his mother's and her importunity had the paroxysms of rage. According to the laws, he was the one to be taken to the mental hospital. Though, he was her only child and she always failed to let him go. She went to the policemen on her knees and beseeched them not to take her boy:

Have mercy on me, – she said unaware that her life was ruined mercilessly a long time ago. The furious neighbors had no desire to listen to her.

Take him away, just take, it's unbearable...- they cried with one voice.

She was a woman of small stature, say, a meter and thirty. Her son was tall, about two meters in height. When they were in a good mood they often walked along the road leading to the market hand in hand. Sometimes they went to the chemist's shop. They talked calmly on their way back too. The tiny woman grasped the palm of Ilusha who was four times taller than his mother and seemed to be pulling him along.

She was a poet. Those who had read the poetry said that it was almost like the one by Rustaveli or Shakespeare. But the disease that her son had been suffering from and the manner of living made her stand the agonizing situation.

Gigla was the next one to wake up in the court. He used to go somewhere early in the morning. He was always well-dressed. He worked in the private sector and there was nothing strange about his zeal to get up early to get the salary that was not bad really. The young single had no one to keep but his own self. He was a good master of his and had to work hard for it. He used to come home Late at night with a huge bag full of provisions.

The third and the most exotic one in the sequence was a woman of the Ossetian origin. She came to the tap always gloomy, put a pail under it and started to babble with a somber face. Over and over again she cursed someone whom she had been aimed at. She started with cursing the Georgian who had been taking care of the lonely widow suffering from hypertension. She was eighty-five years old. When she was fed up with giving them the damns, she crawled into her flat stealthily. It was a box room right under the stairs.

All the tenants of the court followed one another after the four persons. Some of them started up their engines, others ran to buy some bread, and young parents took their kids to school or nursery school. Maya, a young granny with a model's habitus used to take her grandchild to Mushtaidi Park to breathe some fresh air produced by the coniferous trees.

Years ago somebody lugged a big stone into the court (no one knows who did it even now) and put it in front of Gigla's room. There was nothing to sit on in the court. Gigla came back in the evening. He took the enormous stone having a chair shape for something strange, looked at it for a while (who on earth dared put it over there). He dragged it to Temo's door and went home quite satisfied with what he'd done. Next morning the man's wife unwilling to see all the neighbors sitting and making noise right at her door hired a worker and took the wanderer chair to the street.

That was not the end of the nomadic fortune of the chair. Someone brought it into the court again and put it in front of the place where Achiko Tavadze lived.

Some people have all the luck and Diana was the one who had the luck to spend mornings and nights sitting on the stone chair smoking a cigar after another. She talked with people coming into the court and out of it. She used to talk about the things that had been going on within the courtyard and throughout the country. There were just eighteen families living within the area surrounded with their rooms. They were all of different professions: a scientist, an artist and an ordinary craftsman.

Iza, a small girl weighed just thirty-five kilos. She looked like a child in the fifth form. Diana was all a hundred and ten kilos and called her a chick. When her illness was finally diagnosed Iza fully recovered and put on some weight. In the morning and in the evening she used to run up to the second floor breathlessly to have a chat with a film director Nino. They spoke about poetry and art. Nino and Iza used to drink mugs of coffee together.

They had their own doc in the court. They just needed one. Lamara Topuria was a doctor in charge of any case. She was a general practitioner, cardiologist, ophthalmologist, gynecologist and a surgeon. She was good in any of the medical fields and had too many patients due to her humane nature. Maybe it seems a bit strange but she treated the people for their illnesses for free.

Gia was the one among them who had a bloodhound. It was clever enough to watch over the court. If any of the neighbors was late the dog always sat at the gate waiting for the latecomer. It went to sleep just when all the eighteen families were on hand.

Granny Nana pampered their winsome girl Elene. A toy computer, a Barbie's house and what not…She never lost sight of her granny when the woman had to get her pension. And the granny used to spend all her money just to please the kid.

Nathia, the psychologist spent all the time in receiving and seeing off her patients. She was a true telepathist with too many abilities.

When Nadya hang her linen upon the line the children could not go out to play. She stood in the very middle of the court with a big wooden staff in her hand and cried out:

Don't dare hit it with the ball! I'll show you! – She did not stop abusing the people till the sunset. She took the linen off only after the sundown and the kids used to go out with hubbub.

One day Diana came out to the balcony and felt some unusual smell. It was choking. She decided to make it out what it could be and stepped out. The picture was rather strange. The court was covered with a puff of smoke and the people over there were all in confusion. They all were calling Iveta. The flat belonging to the woman and her son was burning. The smoke was just taking the noise to the firmament.

They had put their hands to the ears for it was impossible to stand the noise produced by the water engines. They were crying clamorously:

Help us! Help! – There were twelve fire-fighting vehicles that had gathered at Iveta's house at the same time. The firemen who got into the flat from the roof were astonished at her conduct:

Iveta had sat down right at the windowsill and was singing joyfully: "Flare flames and flare flames, glitter, glitter, glitter"…She was not going to come out and the firemen had to force her out where she started to scream and call her son:

Ilusha, Come out! Lida, come! Valeri…- then she cried again mourning over her son her husband and her parents who had gone long ago. – My Ilusha has burnt, - cried the woman.

She was taken to the mental home. Her son had been over there. The door that was left unburned was boarded up.

One morning she appeared at the house unexpectedly. She had gone out of the hospital secretly. She came afoot. She rustled at the locked door for a long time and finally burst into the room. When she saw the burnt walls her sanity came back to her. She remembered Diana and Nino and Nathia and Lamara. She came to each of the women and apologized for she had not seen them since the time. Suddenly she remembered her son and went crazy again. The neighbors called an ambulance and took her to the asylum again. That was the end incident with her.

When they were putting her into the car something dropped out into the mud from her bag. Temo ran to the thing and picked it up. It was a thick note-book full of marvelous poems. They were all happy for they knew she was the author of the wonderful rhymes. Naira standing in the center of the court read them in a loud voice. They had all gathered and were listening to her carefully. Their thoughts were about one and the same. The woman who had written the magnificent lines had never lived a quiet and happy life. The next day Temo took the threadbare and yellowed note-book to a publishing house and a month later a wonderful collection was on sale.

- Talent, it's here…and your royalties. – He stretched out another hand carrying the money. - Congratulations, Aunt Iveta! - He held out the book to the woman: your book!

Iveta looked down at the book angrily and shouted at the man:

- I am not mad! They took my Ilusha…

- My God! – said the woman in Russian and eventually, Temo realized that the author of the miraculous poetry had nothing in common with the real life and especially with the VERSE.

The lost button

The unexpected leave of her father was a true shock for the girl. She used to cry at night and often failed to fall asleep. She wanted to hug her dad and listen to the fairy tales told by him. He helped her with her studies and watched TV with her. The two always read books together… and now she had not seen him for some months… She can see him too rarely. It makes her heart full of pain and she often tries to cry the pain out of the heart. He has taken nothing but the notebook. And the shirt in the wardrobe with the pungent smell that has turned into a scent for her makes Ann remember her parent. She often takes the shirt off the peg just to feel herself close to dad.

Ann took the shirt out of the wardrobe and went to bed. When she put it against her breast a small button scratched her face. She looked down to the button and remembered how dad once took her to the zoo. At a merry-go-round he lost a button then. She promised to find it for him. She rummaged through the leaves that had already fallen down of trees eager to please the man who had been asking her for quite long to leave the button alone. Yes, she was really happy then. Thinking of the past the girl gave a sign in the bed. Even the sounds of the clock ticking away the time made the recollections come up to the mind. When the tales were over, dad always looked at the clock and said: it's ten o'clock, dear, it's time to go to bed for you now! She hated that clock and the ticking for she wanted to listen to another tale of teddy bears and ogres… It was such a fun. She put the shirt even closer to the heart and fell asleep.

When the girl got fifteen she started to think about an actor's career. Soon she decided to get a film director. She saw too many films then. In the period they showed a new movie at the Tbilisi motion picture theatre. Ann rang around her friends to go to the cinema together. She left a note for her mother and went out of the house.

The impression was really immense. When coming out of the crowded showing room she accidently bumped into a boy. When the youngster turned just to make up an excuse, she got pale. It was such an unexpected meeting. The boy that she'd got acquainted with at a holiday camp had grown up somehow and the eyes, the expressive glare of them had turned into something even deeper and wiser. Some years ago she liked the boy very much. No, she was in love with him. When she came back from the camp she used to think about and dream of him, though time had gained the upper hand over the dreams and she forgot the guy. He was glad to see her and they had a nice talk then. Finally he took the telephone number and promised to ring her up. They said good-bye above the metro station. The chance made her really happy. She cheerfully told her friend about the camp and hardly managed to hide the joy that the meeting with Lasha had made her experience that day. She talked without a stop. One might easily have thought that all the people in the street were her company.

In the morning when she went to school she was so very happy. At noon a friend of her father's called and told Elena about Zurab's sudden death. The woman was just taken aback. The first thing that the remembered then was her daughter. "Thank God! She's gone to school and knows nothing"! – thought the woman. She truly mourned over the man. Though they had been divorced for a long time, they were friends. And the girl, she loved her father so very much. How was she going to tell Ann about the death? It was his heart that failed.

When Zurab was interred her classmates did not go back a step from Ann and encouraged her as if they had been grown up enough for the things like that. She grieved deeply and cried all the time for the man that she'd just lost was her father and her friend. She could hardly imagine her life without him. They seldom met each other but she knew for sure, he was somewhere in the city and would always come to the aid there and then.

Sitting alone on the balcony Ann thinks of the day in summer when she left for a village in Svaneti mounts with her friends. They were in the eights form when one of their classmates asked some children to come to his bower. They all had some money and Ann was the only exception for mom had failed to lend some 200 rubles for her. In the end Ann made up her mind to call her dad. He never failed to understand her and she could always rely upon him. She went to the other room without uttering a word and phoned Zurab. He was really glad to hear her from the receiver.

-What's up with you, maybe you need something? - asked the man.

- Dad, oh, dad, please give me some two hundred rubles, please find them for me! And don't tell anyone about that! Let it be our secret, please!

Zurab wondered what was the thing that she needed for the money so badly and when Ann told him about the plans he asked what was the date and the time scheduled for the train to leave. He promised to bring her money without hesitation or doubt.

He called her on Thursday. "Dear, remember we read "The Life of Kartli". Please read every single page of the book with attention. Do your best and study as much as you can, honey"! – said the man and hang up the receiver.

Yes, Ann remembered the book. She remembered they read it. There was nothing strange about her father's words. She knew he wanted her to be a well-educated girl.

Ann started preparing for the trip. She had never spent her holidays in a mountainous village. In a sports bag she put all the books and clothes she wanted to have there. She also took a camera to take some pictures over there. It was a great pleasure for her to take up photography. Views of the mountainous part of the world would be a nice opportunity for a photographer. She was happy, really very, very happy counting days and hours before the departure. Each day when she came home from school she waited for her father to ring her up. And she was the first one to rush to the door when there was someone knocking against it.

It was Saturday night. Though, he hadn't come yet. She thought he did not want to give their secret away. "Yes, he'll bring me the money at the station", - thought the girl and fell asleep with no worry. In the morning she could not force herself make a step away from the window. When her friends called Ann to come down from the yard, she thought about her father and the railway station again and ran down the stairs with mom in a quite joyful mood. She stood there folded in her mother's arms and finally said good-bye to her.

There were too many people fusing around at the platform. Ann looked round the place trying to find him, though in vein. She came running up to a public telephone and tried to call him. She dialed the number in such a troubled manner but…there was no voice heard from the receiver. Hence, she could hear her own heart pulsating so frequently and irregularly. Then she realized that it was aunt Nutsa calling her loudly and strictly. She was almost to disappear from the platform but aunt Nutsa grasped her hand and pulled her into the car. The abashed girl who was shivering all over the body stood there among her merry friends who could not understand what was up with Ann. She was angry and nervously bit her nails.

In a fortnight they all came back to the city. They had all missed their parents and were busy telling the stories of the village.

No, no, she does not want to think about the summer… Ann jumped up to her feet. She had to do the homework with her small brother. She is a high achiever and can help the boy.

The next day Lasha called her. Well, it was a rather unexpected call. No doubt, it was good news for Ann. She invited the boy over to her place. Mom had prepared a cake for them. There were some of her friends too and they had just a good time that evening. Before leaving Lasha whispered in her ear that he was taking his papers to her school right the next day. Her eyes sparkled with happiness, though she turned pale. It was not easy to control the pleased smile.

When the bell rang the class teacher came into the room and said for everybody to hear: "We have a new pupil"! She turned to the door and led a stately, green-eyed boy in. The enraptured girl just cried something out. She smiled to Lasha from the distance and only afterwards approached him with her friend Eka. She seized his hand and introduced him to the class.

Two years passed. Ann is in the tenth form now. She does her best and can even debate with her teachers. The discussions with the historian are especially hot. They argue about facts and developments. Once a certain date stirred up such a dispute between them that the girl was surprised by the liberty she dared to take then of saying things that she'd told. When the lessons were over the form master started to talk about the banquet planned to be held at a prestigious restaurant in the uptown. They had already ordered a dinner for twenty-seven youngsters.

At the break Lasha took her hand. He said she had to sit in his car and dance only with him during the evening. The girl looked at the boy all brightened up and thought about things that slightly differed.

On the way home she thought of the money that she needed so badly for the banquet. There was no chance for mom to give her the sum and dad, yah, he was not alive. Would he have given her it this time? Maybe…It would have been a present truly nice.

Mom was busy working at the kitchen. Her brother was playing with a ball on the balcony. Ann took "The Life of Kartli" from a bookshelf and made herself comfortable in the easy chair. She could not wait to check up the date she had argued about with the teacher today. She looked through the contents. When she opened the book she just stiffened. It was a find that would have easily make one dumbfounded. She looked with dilated eyes at the note and some money that had been kept in the book. She tried to touch the paper with her trembling hand. She opened the folded up message and read: "My dearest, take the money and have a good time! Always keep in mind that your dad loves you so much"! Ann got pale in her face. Tears bleared her eyes. Yes, those were the tears of sorrow. She counted the money, then put the note to the breast and just burst into tears. The girl grieved about her father and the fact that she blamed him sometime for something that he had never been guilty of. She remembered the day when he phoned and asked her to read the book two years ago. She remembered the book left on the table. Yes, she thought that it was her mother who left "The Life of Kartli" over there then. She wished she had never thought the things that she had in her mind then. Ann cried. She did not understand him and it pained the girl. She felt she was guilty towards her dad. Begging his pardon she realized it was impossible to really apologize to him for he was dead.

When she heard her daughter's voice Ann's mother came running into the room. "What's up, honey? Why are you crying, please tell me"! - repeated the woman trying to shake something out of the girl.

Ann hugged her mom as if seeking consolation in her arms. "It was not his fault...it's me, me, mom! I slandered him...I loved dad so much... He was right"! - sobbed out the girl.

Though she could not understand what Ann was about she listened to her with sympathy and said lovingly: "Yes, my dear, mom's here with you. Good girl, good girl...calm down, please"! It was not easy for Elena to hide the embarrassment caused by the scene.

Finally Ann fell asleep. Elena covered the girl with a quilt and stood up. She saw the banknotes scattered over there. First she did not know what to do with the money. When she stooped down to pick up the papers she noticed the folded up message. She had seen the hand before. She read the letter and wondered who could have written it. She fell down on the chair. Now she knew for sure what the thing that had disturbed her daughter was. When would the girl absolve herself from the blame... Thinking of the girl's feelings the woman still kept the money in her hands in a manner one might think she'd never seen anything of the kind. It was a symbol of a woe, a forerunner and still something very necessary and needed. She muttered: "It's nothing, absolutely nothing as against the misery and the spiritual values".

The girl who had steeped in an untroubled slumber seemed to be quite quiet. The sum brought by her father promised her to have a good time at the banquet.

The ominous melody

I could not leave the window open at night. It was awfully hot in summer but I preferred to sleep with the windows closed for I felt more safe so. I used to bolt the windows before going to bed and opened them in the morning. My husband always told me: - Don't be afraid, open the windows! Though, I dreaded to think that he could get in through the windows of the ground floor. It was so exhausting.

It was a method of self-defense. The fear had been torturing me for years. I left one of the windows first…Then I opened two ones and finally I forgot about the terror. We left the windows open even when we went to the country to have the rooms aired out when we'd come back.

Giorgi liked sitting on a windowsill. He used to sit over there and waved his hand to the cars moving along the street: – Hi, guys! Good-bye uncles! - He raised his little hands and made us laugh. He had a very, very small red chair to crawl up to the window. He dragged it to the window and stood on it over there. Then he managed to jump up to the opening and smiled to get in contact with the world surrounding him. He was a good-natured boy and loved almost everyone. One could see it at first sight. Any car was a "gingia" for him. So we had "father's gingia", a "gingia" of granny and a boy's "gingia", i.e. a car belonging to someone else.

The girl practised music and used to play one and the same melody as if harping on one string. I played the piano myself. I had some compositions of my own. I also wrote the texts for them. The neighbors were so used to the musical sounds coming out of the apartment that when they could not hear them they thought we had gone to the country.

It took just an hour to get to our village. We used to go there almost each Sunday. We had a wonderful orchard there with all the strawberries, cherry plums, apples, grapes, pears, peaches, tangerines and different sorts of pomegranates. Giorgi had a huge toy car in the yard and there was a swing hung for Eka too. We used to sit on it in turns.

One Friday when we were all ready to leave for our village the car broke down. My husband decided to go by bus and we had to be at home. Giorgi had thrown himself at his dad and was not going to let the man go. Finally the man freed himself from the boy and we all accompanied him to the end of the road. We were sad when we got back. The children settled down at the TV and I went to the piano. I played long and performed popular variety songs. It was a surprise even for me for I had been sitting and playing for so long. Then I took the children out to play in front of the house. I was cheerless that day. I felt lonely and the feeling of responsibility for my children had burdened my mind. I had never been alone. There was always someone by my side and by the side of my children. Later on I realized that I sang too long and loudly just because I was full of desire to conceal the melancholy.

I was slow in going home. I wanted to have supper with the children and go to bed earlier. An old neighbor stopped me at the door of our apartment and told me about her past once again. I managed to get rid of the woman and we came in. I put the kettle on the gas heater hastily. Giorgi fell asleep without his supper. He slept right on the ottoman. Eka had some bread and butter with her tea. They were deep asleep when they started to show "Pretty Woman". – I have to see the film, - I said and sat down comfortably at the TV. I had some fruit in front of me, that Adessa grapes and pears. And I drank some cold milk from a big crystal glass.

The film put me in a good mood. I wished all the inhabitants of the planet the same love and before going to bed checked the door again. Both doors were locked and bolted. A left a small light bulb burning in the hallway as I usually did for I did not like the darkness. It lit the whole apartment gently and I could easily see the children. I looked down at the watch. It was fifteen minutes to two. I took off the clothes hurriedly and went to bed. I fell asleep instantly.

I heard some unexceptional music right at my ears. I jumped up or, to be more exact, sat in my bed. Almost a minute passed before I realized where I was and from where the sounds of the music were coming. When I finally regained control over myself I first remembered that my husband was not at home. We were alone—me and my children. Though, there was someone playing a strange and pleasant melody pattering his fingers on the keys of the piano standing in the drawing-room.

I was paralyzed. The melody repeated several times. The slow tipping changed by some harsh striking was a sign for me that there was someone in the room. I did not know who it was but there could be no doubt that we had got into trouble. I knew for sure that it was not a dream. I came to the children's bed immediately and looked at them sleeping with a deep, profound sleep. If I made up my mind to enter the drawing-room with the piano in it I would have to come out of the bedroom door. I was shaking all over with fear. I had turned my back to the room and could not even look in the direction. I thought who the man could be. I had already imagined the stranger: it was a man, a man and no one else...I could not see his face for he had turned his back to me...The piano was set against me. Though, I knew he was dressed in black. The man with a stout constitution seemed to have black hair and beard. His hands had to be large and his expression had to be strict. Who would ever guess what the reason of his visit was or what he was going to do next. I had to forestall with an attack. I had just to do something. I wiped the sweat from my forehead, took a deep sigh and got ready for acting. I was the only defender of the helpless children and I had no right to do nothing.

But how did he slip in? I had closed the door carefully. – I was rater disturbed by the thoughts. There are big, fine gratings made of iron on the windows. It's impossible for anyone to steal into the apartment. And who's the man sitting at the piano in the sitting-room? Is it a ghost? A phantom? So much the worse...The devil...A strange feeling pierced something inside me. Oh, all the doubts and hesitation...Maybe he came in when I took the children out to play, - I thought and got even more afraid. He was here when I was watching the movie happily and when I put my head calmly on the pillow and fell asleep...Oh, Lord, save us! - I said and summoned my strength. I stood up noiselessly.

moved to the cupboard. There was an old sporting gun belonging to my grandfather sometime. My eldest brother used to fowl in the country with the gun. I remember he once said: - Wanna shoot? – I was so glad… I ran up and dashed to him. When he passed the gun to me it appeared to be too heavy for me and I let it fall. Then he carried it for me and helped me to pull the trigger. The noise made me so very glad and happy. I imagined I was a hero and I wanted to do more. I have been dreaming to go to the mountains and hunt after a bear since the day. Though, I've never had a chance to fulfill the wish.

I plucked up my courage, put the jeans on and came to the cupboard without making noise. I opened the door. It was hard for me to touch the gun hunging on a peg. I took it and started to move out of the room with those stealthy steps. I looked at the children again. They had been deep asleep. The only wish I had was to have the kids somewhere else in safety. I did not worry about myself. All absorbed in the thoughts I tried to sneak up to the victim. And now, I'm too close to the door. I'll open it and see the man dressed in black. The man has black hair and beard and the expression of his face is too severe. His hands are just enormous and when he touches the keys they make the melody that is menacing and beautiful at the same time.

And the strike upon the keys again, and the odd melody and the patience that I have already run out of make me rush to the door and open it. Just two leaps and I reached the piano. Look! It was impossible to believe one's own eyes. I've never thought of such an end. I hardly realized what was going on. I could not understand whether it was true or I had just seen a dream. It was difficult for me to carry the gun. I felt relief and was to drop the gun. A cat running up and down along the keys had its claw hammered between them. He could not free himself. When the cat saw me, he was so frightened that started to walk again making some disorderly sounds with the rest three paws. The sight made a smile leak through the features of my face. I was so glad to see the grey cat that I even patted its fluffy hair. Then I began to release the claw. He seemed to have understood what was going on and did not bite me. It was not easy to take the claw out of the keyboard. When he was free he turned to me. His eyes were asking my pardon for stealing through the window without any permission. He seemed to have the blues for threatening me. There were too many things concealed in the gaze. He looked at me with the motley eyes for a while and suddenly jumped out of the open window. I came to the window and looked out. He was running in such a manner as if there was someone willing to catch him. The cat seemed to understand everything just like men. I closed the window and smiled unwittingly again…

I had left the piano open at night. Probably it was the milk smell that drove the cat into the house. I was drinking some milk when I was watching TV standing at the window. It's my fault only and there was no problem with the grey musician.

I have been seeking for the cat since the time to treat him with a bowl of milk.

The three repentant hearts

The boys turned at the end of the street. The policemen failed to catch sight of them. They set off the alarm and started to overrun throughout the streets in the vicinity. They all just vanished as if the ground had swallowed them up. At the moment somebody shot at Zaza from the attic of an apartment and wounded him in the shoulder. No one could understand from where the shot was made. People gathered around the wounded. Someone had already called emergency. This was the third time he was wounded and he knew for sure who had done it. His buddies wounded them more than once. He always got off easy himself. To make a long story short it were Zaza and Levan who had to stay at the hospital heavily wounded by turns. Though, the Lord in the Highest did not want them to die and they got back to their families quite recovered.

The trouble was caused by an insignificant thing. In the street overcrowded with people somebody stroke against Zaza. He turned and swore in a loud voice. The women involuntarily cried out and put their palms against their mouths. A man standing nearby put on airs and pointed to the women and children politely. Zaza cast a menacing glance at Levan and swore again. Then he continued his way and suddenly felt a cuff from the behind that was so strong that there was a buzzing in his ears. The fallen man got up at once buttoning up his shirt...Then he turned round all of a sudden and punched the "mentor" right into his face. They beat each other until the policemen came. They happened to be quite fortunate even then. The police always failed to catch them. And they always managed to disappear immediately.

A week later Zaza came to Levan's district. He couldn't find him for three days and finally saw him in the Park of Vere. At the end of the park, in a remote corner one could hear the voices of some people quarreling and swearing over there. Then Zaza pulled out a knife from his pocket, made just a swing and concealed himself. He had cut Levan's face. The blood gushed from the wounded cheek and ran down to his breast. He took his shirt off and put it down on the wound. He stood over there for a few minutes and then dragged himself along the path to reach the road.

One more week passed and now Levan's friends beat Zaza almost to death. He spent six month at the hospital. The enmity seemed to have no end. For four years they had been at loggerheads with each other and scuffled every single month with all the pals they had.

Zaza was an orphan. His aunt, a sister of his father's did her best to bring up the nephew. He had a talent for painting. He was in the forth form when his teacher called the aunt and told that the talented boy had to go in for painting. Mary tried to entreat him, though all in vain... He painted just when he wanted to paint, when he felt he had to do so.

Mary had promised her brother to bring the boy up as her own son and she never forgot the promise. It was her vow. When he left his school she brought him a car. He was always dressed fashionably, always spent his holidays at health resorts and always had good time with his old friends.

He got married when he was sixteen years old and used to leave the girl at home all alone. He was always here and there, always busy with his own business. The poor girl just ran way. Shortly after that he married another girl. She was too pretty but she lived with him for five months only and ran away too. Her husband had no time for her. He could not lose touch with the world surrounding him and it was impossible for the young girl to lead the isolated life at home.

He kept a pistol in a drawer. It belonged to a criminal authority sometime. One of his friends gave it to him as a birthday present. The gory handgun had been used to kill too many people. He loved it even more than his own self. He treasured it up.

The strife seemed to be led to its end. They were both tired of it. They had not seen each other for a year but there was no guarantee that they would not quarrel again on meeting. It was their position to fight to the finish.

One day a middle-aged man sat down on a yard bench just by his side. Zaza looked mockingly at the man dressed in a cassock. He wanted to tell the man to change the seat but something made him stop...All the ecclesiastical traditions, priestly vestments and the lifestyle always made him smile ironically. He took the people for fools who had never been aware of the pleasures of the world. He made up his mind to ask the man why he had preferred the pointless and dull hieratic life to the fun and freedom. It seemed to be better to respond to one's heart and live in comfort. Though, he looked into the man's eyes the asked him sadly and with some notes of sympathy in his tone: Do you believe in him?

Father Giorgi talked easily. It was so pleasant to the ear. He said that the ways of the Lord lead us to the eternity and the repentance is the only way to survive. One could see that Zaza was listening just for the sake of propriety. He was impatient to go away from the place but he felt as if there was someone repeating: - Stay over there, don't go! – And he kept sitting there. It was a test of endurance. He listened like a captive, a humble servant. It was the Almighty talking to him in the person of Father Giorgi. He remembered all the believers with the Bibles in their hands that he met in the streets now. The legislation that worked before (the Communist order) used to prohibit visiting churches. The people had already learned much about the God. They had rushed to the churches. They all confessed their sins and learned by heart the prayers and psalms.

Something changed in Zaza's life that day. You'd never see him in the street. He spent all his time at home and wet out only on Sundays. He was earnest and polite and greeted his acquaintances calmly. They watched at him walking away from them but no one could realize what could be the reason of the sharp change.

It was a frosty morning in January. The snow had covered the road in one night. The footprints had worked the way to the temple. He stood by the door of the church shivering all over because of the cold or praying too wholeheartedly. He was wholly absorbed in the tacit praying. He seemed to be so sincere that one might have taken him for a monk. After the conversation with Father Giorgi he came to the Church. It was the confessor who had made him decide to go there once in his life at least. When he approached the parvis the Spirit of God touched him and he began to cry. The priest advised him to get ready for the confession. Now he had nothing in common with the past, with the streets and the criminal life that he had considered to be something absolute.

He spent three years in praying and fasting. The confession and receiving had turned into something ordinary for him. He did not come out of his room from where the sounds made by his saw and file could be heard. He used to cut something over there too. He did not let anyone into the room and the aunt kept silent. She just thanked the God for his conversion to faith. Some months later he brought something covered with some satin out of his room and told his aunt that he was going to stay at the church that night. He stepped along the way leading to the shrine.

Quite many people had come to the church since the morning. They christened some children over there. Three kids had started screaming almost simultaneously.

The Lord repeated something to Zaza who stood on his knees at the icon of Jesus. His voice was so pacifying and kind. Zaza had a candle in his hand lit to confess the sins. He looked into the eyes of the icon while his own ones were filled with tears. The memories of his deeds had arisen. He had remembered everything and he felt that he had to listen to the God telling him about something. He stopped praying and heard distinctly: - "Love thy neighbour as thyself"! – were the words repeated by the calm and mysterious voice that he had never heard before. He automatically turned his face to the place where the infant baptism was administered. Among the children standing over there he saw a face that he could easily recognize. The face had turned to him and was looking into his eyes too. The man had a candle in his hand and was made to turn to him by the God's word.

Suddenly he felt a lump in the throat. It was not him, just somebody cried out instead of him: - Levan! Brother! – Levan's face was shining with happiness. He was moving towards Zaza. They met at the miracle-working icon and hugged each other unwittingly. There was a scar left after the wound on Levan's face. Zaza hung his head in shame and started to murmur something out. He looked at the sore again. - I'm sorry, Levan! - He groaned. The feelings of regret and forgiveness had left their imprints on their features. The hymn sung to the God could get to the bottom of one's heart and filled the people who had come with the genius of Love. In the parvis the trees and bushes covered with snow could remind of the garden of Eden.

He asked his aunt, who had brought him up, to pardon him for what he had done again and again. Mary used to walk up the way leading to the temple with her heart that had turned into a repentant one as well. She went to the place to make her own confession. She had to confess the anger and grievance that she had nursed against her nephew for years.

Zaza Christened as Elizbar was consecrated a nun and had moved to his cell forever. As for Levan, he comes to the temple standing nearby each Sunday. Elizbar can see him from the distance. He is happy for he can experience the greatest feeling of love.

The snowfall had been heavy that year. The monks found a huge heap at the door of the cell. They never closed the door of the Shrine and the wind had closed it that night. They threw the snow off and stepped in. The picture was just striking, miraculous as the Crucifixion…

Nun Elizbar had put his body tightly against the Crucifixion of Jesus Christ with his arms spread wide. The extreme cold of the night had frozen him over there.

The unforgettable apple taste

She has not gone to the cemetery for five years. She knew too many followers of different religions. She was embarrassed. They all said things that originally differed. Some of them proved that all the visits to the cemeteries were absolutely meaningless for the dead person and his rotten body. Others affirmed the contrary of the statement. They said that one had to go to the graves quite often and look after them. They emphasized that she was to pay her last respects to the dead and visit his grave. To cut a long story short, in that state of confusion she did not go to the cemetery, did not lit candles and did not pray for her father.

Five years passed. She did not want to go to the country that summer. She used to have a longing for the village. It was too hot that the city was almost empty. In the torrid heat she preferred to stay in the mounts. She packed up all her belongings and went to the country. When the minibus reached the village it had already become dark. The cold breeze happened to be pleasant for the girl sweltered with the sultriness of the city. She lied down on a couch and fell deep asleep. Her mother was so happy that sat up the night. She looked at her dormant girl and cooked different dishes to treat her properly the next day. She remembered her childhood and was always puttering in the kitchen.

She was twelve years old when her father bought a small TV for her. She was so glad that she could not sleep a whole week. She decorated her room, put some wild flowers into a vase, placed the TV near her bed and curtained the window as if she was afraid someone would look into the room from outside. But there was a vast forest full of firs and pines behind the glasses. She used to switch the TV on before going to bed and watched movies. Though, she always failed to see a film from beginning to its end for she always fell asleep. Mom usually came into the room noiselessly and switched off the TV. Her father, a man who was strict for everyone was so softhearted towards the girl. He always tried to do his best to make the child happy.

Are you going to stay here for a long time, dear? - asked her mother the next day. The answer made the woman gloomy. – Maybe you can stay for a bit long, – she said. – That depends, mom! But if you want me be by your side too much, sure, I won't go, - She embraced her mother and went up to the first floor.

The windows were open in her room. She could see the orchard full of fruit-trees. The branches of an apple-tree were now rushing against the window glass. The tree made her remember the childhood. Once she had a contest with her brother. They competed with each other in eating apples. The elder brother cheated her that she'd grow up a centimeter with each eaten fruit. She hated apples, though she wanted to be a big girl and took a bite after another. She even spat up. But her brother took her to a wall and pointed to the old line made with a pencil on the wall. - You've grown too much, - said the boy. She used to be so glad that she dashed to her brother and kissed him. - How good it is that you've taught me, I'll eat ten apples every–single day.

One day she washed ten apples with her tiny hands and put them in front of her. She ate the apples and smiled joyfully. She thought she would catch up with her cousin Nelly and grow up even taller than the girl soon. She was all smiles but when she started to eat the fourth apple it was so terrible that she decided never to have one. She hates apples now for she can feel the taste of the apples eaten against her will.

Days passed rapidly and Nia all absorbed in her own memories did not realize that it was the time for her to go. One more week and she had to go to work. She suffered from sleeplessness at night. Why cannot I sleep? - She thought and spent nights reading and writing.

She could not close her eyes that night. She tossed and turned in the bad. Finally she got tired of it all and got up angrily. She went to the drawing-room. She was a writer. She grasped some blank papers. An idea struck her and in a few minutes she had already written some pages. Then she looked up as if she had remembered something. Right above her head there was her father's photograph hanging on the wall. He is frowning on the picture. Maybe he was angry when he took the photo. It was the day of his bearing out when they enlarged it. Nia was furious. Why, he looks better on other photos. But mom wanted the one and she did not say a word. It has been hanging over there for five years. He looked right into her eyes. His gaze was so strange. She was afraid and tried to stand up but she was ashamed of herself. She forced herself to go on with writing.

The fear, the desire to stand up and the failure to act had been mixed up in her mind. How difficult it was to experience the fear. It was an unbearable feeling. Only the recollections of her father's temper made her sit over there. – A shame on you! Afraid of me?!- He'd say. And she remained firm and kept sitting, though all willing to leave the place. She could do nothing else.

Suddenly she heard some noise from the ceiling. Something fell down on the floor with all its strength. It was black. She recognized the color when it was still in the air. She saw the place where it fell down, just a meter from her. It instantly disappeared. She jumped to his feet and peered at the place where the thing fell with that rattling sound. There was nothing left on the floor painted in red.

The next day she heard the same noise in the orchard. In the evening the noise repeated. They were sitting together with her mother in the drawing room. When the thing fell down the din made the women jump up again. Nia burst out crying and told her mom about that night. They kept silent for they were amazed and threatened.

Nia thought it was her father who had got angry with her for she did not go to the cemetery. There was a true tangle in her head stirred up by the protestant teaching. And the country had been an Orthodox one. She decided to go to the churchyard. She went to the photograph and looked into her father's eyes. - Dad, I know it's you who makes the noise! I know what you're about! Forgive me, please... She asked her mother to give her some candles, wine, bread and cheese, put them on a dish and went up the road leading to the cemetery.

In the evening dad was smiling to her. There had been no noise since the day and she had never felt the fear…She wondered at the fact for she knew that the face from the photograph always used to look at them too strictly. She had to go to the city in three days. Nia came into the room frequently and looked at the picture in stealth. Maybe was an apparition. But there were no doubts that the man was smiling to her. Finally she decided to ask her mother.

It turned out that the woman could see just the same. She said her husband smiled from the picture like he did when he was either glad with something or satisfied with the deep-rooted traditions cherished in the family.

The ward of lucky stars

He passed through the corridor with the quick steps so very usual for him; stopped at the ward 13 and half-opened the door slowly. Thea set down and set her eyes on the doc. She gazed on him full of expectation and smiled. The doctor measured her blood pressure, looked through the results of the blood tests and checked her body. It was obvious that he was amazed to see the weak and delicate girl. Yes, he was charmed and amazed. "It's OK", - said the doc, patted her on the head and left the room.

The girl was astonished at the man's conduct. Though she was pleased with the cordiality. She had dealt with medical persons since she was a child, but had never seen a doctor so very thoughtful and nice.

Thea looked up at the sky through the window. The space above her could easily remind one of a canvas painted by an artist where all the creatures of the Universe were made of clouds. She could not tear herself away from the picture of the moving cloudy bodies. It was a typical morning in June, though it was not hot at all. The weather was dull and warm. She was unusually joyful but the weakness did not let her really realize the feeling of joy. Deep in thought she did not even notice the physician who had come back. She sat on the bed immediately.

How are you? – asked the doctor pushing up a chair to the bed. – Have you had your breakfast yet?

Cannot eat boiled fish, the taste is just terrible, - said the girl with some obstinacy in her voice. She smiled to the doc as if she was going to beseech him to do something for her. The tenderness of the girl made Davit Kharadze think of a thing that made him leap up from the chair as if someone had caught him red-handed. In confusion he failed to fix his eyes at a point.

Eat some meat then, - said the man as if the words could serve him as a way out form the embarrassment. – You have some protein deficiency and that's not good.

Oh, boiled meat, it's rather good. She seemed to be glad. The girl tried to get up from the bed with the glints of joy burning in her green eyes. She failed.

OK, have a rest, - said Davit to Thea smilingly and went out of the room as quickly as he usually did. She tossed and turned in the bed for quite a long time and finally fell deep asleep with her face put against the wall. In the morning a nurse awakened Thea to give her an injection. The woman tried to talk to her.

You are so beautiful. Why are you suffering from hepatitis? And the form is complicated…

Don't know, - said the girl shrugging her shoulders.

He is a professional. Don't be afraid! You know, I have been thinking of you since the day you came here. I have already seen you somewhere. Where do you live?

In Vake district. And you?

In Dighomi. Well, there was a penny for her thoughts. She seemed to be stirred up by some recollections. She stood up and left the ward instantly.

Yes, she had see the nurse…but where?! Right.. It was her… The girl remembered the pallid face of her father… the woman's dilated eyes. The central figure in the memories was her father, a cheerful man whose hair had just started to grow grey.

It happened about fifteen years ago. When she was coming home from school a car nearly ran into her at the turn of the road. There was the woman sitting in her father's car. He uttered a frenzied shriek, broke away from the car, grasped her with his hands and cried out clasping the child in his arms. Thea was probably eleven years old then. She had put her head against her dad's breast. Her own heart was beating rapidly. The man took her by heart. On their way home he bought some chocolate and ice-cream for the girl. She loved it so much. He gave her even some money and asked not to tell mom anything of what had already happened. She looked at the man in wide-eyed astonishment for she could not realize what was the reason of making secrets. However, the girl nodded.

Later the puzzle still turned out to be unveiled. Her mother saw the couple at the Rustaveli Theatre with the tickets in their hands. There was a row then. She thought for a long time that dad wanted to keep her mother from the impressions dealing with the possible car accident, though no one was exposed to danger now. In truth, the man wanted to keep the adventure in secret. And now the woman is just by her side, she is Thea's own nurse giving her shots twice a day. What a strange thing the human life is.

Dad showed her the woman another time. It happened again and again and the only thing that he asked her was to keep silent. The girl used to be as good as her word. She had already divined who the woman was and did not want to hurt her mom. On the other hand, the silence was an attempt to win the man's confidence.

Now in the sky blue ward her thoughts are about something that differs from the possible cure. Yes, she looks in the direction of the door all waiting for the doc touched with grey. For more than a month she has been witnessing the sunrise from the hospital window and does not even want to be discharged, though the recovery so very uncommon for the patients is obvious. She is absolutely free here, surrounded with warmth, cordiality and care. The heedful doctor has been by her side since the very beginning as if he has had no other patients waiting for him. The attention makes her heart surprisingly happy.

The hospital with all the docs in their smocks and the way of life has turned out to be much more pleasing for Thea than the healthy and primitively simple existence outside the walls. The regard given to her was quite enough to smooth over all the anxiety and troubles.

Once the ward round was over, the Head of the Department asked Davit to come to his office. Sitting in the chair in the manner typical of him the man was moving the glasses with his fingers. He was strict enough and asked the doctor to discharge all the patients who had been at the hospital for a period of time longer than a month. Davit nodded without a word and left the staff lounge.

Davit Kharadze rushed into the ward. He seemed to be exasperated, though the bad mood was so very uncharacteristic of him. "Have to discharge you", - he said in a strict voice that sounded so very unfamiliar and turned back hurriedly. She had never seen Davit in such a bad temper and could hardly realize what the reason of his anger was. She was unaccustomed to things like that. The man who always smiled to her and was so tender had now turned into someone just furious. She stood dumbfounded for a while. She felt low and turned to the bed to cower, though her head started swimming. She lost control over her body and fell down on the edge of the chair.

Davit got back to the ward with a case report in his hand. When he saw the bent body lying on the floor and the bleeding forehead, he grasped the girl like a mad man and looked straight into her face. He was impressed by the site of the long fair hair mixed with the blood puddle right on the floor of the room. She opened her eyes slightly and saw the phantom of the man. The girl tried to smile to him, but she was too exhausted. Thea closed her eyes and fainted again. However the treatment turned out to be quite effective, there were no symptoms of life left on her face. The confused man striding back and forth with the body clasped in his arms had already started to call the personnel clamorously.

It was quite late when she came to consciousness. They tested her blood again. The doctor washed off the blood from the girl's hair and saw the wound on the forehead. He grasped the hand of the patient and took her to the operating room where a surgeon placed some sutures on the injury. Thea looked in the mirror and smiled. The girl who used to be easily frightened and timid was now glad to see the wound and the forehead. When he was by her side there was something pleasant even about the pain.

The nurse appeared in the doorway. The woman stared at the couple silently and the traces of the past started to recollect in her mind. The girl was going home from school when together with Dito they ran across her at the road turning. Her own father nearly crushed into the child. Yes, she was the exact image of her father. The eyes, the forehead… the thoughts made her forget about Davit who was over there. Suddenly she came to her senses, apologized and went away.

She fell asleep right as they gave some injections. Her face was lit with happiness. At midnight she jumped out of the bad as if something had awakened her. There was Davit sitting by her side and carrying her weak fingers in his palms. The girl felt the warmth of the man who was looking at her hands as at something belonging to him and nobody else.

When he went out one of the colleagues told him something about an infirm. He even gave a question to Davit. Though, the man could hear nothing. The astonished physician looked at him and left him right away. Brooding over something Davit went down the stairs. Walking outside the building he looked like one dumb and blind at the same time, who had hardly shaken off a dull conversation with a passerby.

Involuntarily he found himself in her ward again. The girl who was deep asleep did not notice him. He looked at her for some time and then sat down at the head of her bad. It seemed to be impossible; he realized that his marked attention towards the girl was conditioned not by his profession. It was a warm and nice feeling. And I managed to find her", - he thought with a smile covering his face.

Another prescription and a new course of treatment and she was ready to leave the hospital in a week. However, she felt just sadness. She long sat at the window and talked to herself with an inanimate expression. No, she did not want to go and that was a problem. But it was a hospital and no one could stay there forever. She was rather perplexed for she did not know how to avoid the end of the beautiful dream. Tears ran out of her eyes. She did not want anyone to see her in the situation and stood up rapidly. She seized the bag that mom had sent to her and started to take some clothes out of it.

At noon she was dressed in a green brand-new frock with the collar slightly away from the centre. The fair hair slipped down the shoulders like a rain. Her green eyes were burning in ignescent all-absorbing sun-rays. When she was ready to go, they ran into each other in the corridor. Davit failed to hide the feeling of delight and said:

"How very beautiful you are looking, Thea"!

He opened his arms wide and gazed at her fixedly. "Don't discharge me, doc! Don't do it! I don't want to go! Please let me stay here, please"! She put her head against the doc's breast now. Tears were running down her cheeks. Davit tried to calm the girl down, though it was hard to control the smile of happiness… He could embrace and pet his beloved one. The doctor was trying to smooth the hair on the wounded forehead.

In the other end of the corridor the whole staff of doctors, nurses and orderlies was just astonished by what they had a chance to witness then. They were all silent and averted their eyes only when the two looked at them. Davit had forgotten everything that he could ever be concerned about. He was finally free from the ominous loneliness. The fortune made him meet the lovely and kind girl and it did no matter for him what the colleagues could think about him.

His shining face and the smart appearance promised Thea to have many, many days of happiness and surprise. Carrying the tiny palm in his hand he walked along the long terrace leading out of the hospital with steps that were as short as her own ones.

Suddenly he stopped thinking of something from the past. He looked at her finger and smiled. When he was a boy dad took him to Moscow. He liked a ring there. It was a rare piece of adornment costing quite much. There was a precious stone in a gold rim. Dad wondered what for wanted the boy to have the ring. Though, the kid kept silent… The ring has been hidden in the drawer since the time. Maybe he sensed something then…The ring absolutely fitted her small finger.

In the garden, in the shade of enormous poplar trees the morning had started to tell the story of love. Nelly who had leant her elbows on the windowsill was looking at the couple in disguise. The impression of her face was one of a woman looking towards the love that had gone far for good.

The untimely bells

The school campus hooted with the joyful noise of children. The whole essence of the selfless fight was to seize the ball and kick it as far as possible from the close. Suddenly the bell rang and they had to stop playing. Akaki who was forward enough, turned back and called the other boys to go on with the contest when the next break would come.

The renewed game appeared to be even more desperate. All the children looked at Lekso and Akaki, who had already proved themselves as leaders. The violent fight started just to spend time seemed to be going to turn into a serious scuffle. Once Lekso tried to snatch the ball with his foot, Akaki shouldered him and the forceful blow made the boy rush into the huge oak-tree standing in the campus. The boy fell down on the back with his nose bleeding. Akaki looked at him with the gaze typical of a scoffer and passed him by with his shoulder widely spread and proud of the glory.

Lekso was seriously injured. Some children took him to the school doc. The latter examined the boy, treated the wound with alcohol and asked him to stay in bed for some days because of the headache that he was suffering from.

He missed all the lessons that week. He felt his head was aching, though when Mom asked what was up, the boy told that he had fallen down and hurt his nose when playing football.

Then someone called him. The chuckle and the titter through the telephone line made him feel anger. Akasi asked him about his plans dealing with coming to school and the wound on his nose with the cynical tone so very characteristic of him.

It was the most amazing moment of the situation that the boy who was just in the sixth form behaved as a grown man. He decided not to pay attention to Akaki, though in truth he was beside himself with rage and knew it for sure that the opponent should have his way and should necessarily make him lose patience.

On Monday he went to school. Nursing a grievance the boy greeted his class-mates with a smile on his face. When the third lesson was over the form master held a meeting. The children who had almost reached their transition age happened to be extremely aggressive and the pedagogues expressed their resentment. The director was aware of the situation. He called the class teacher and made her answer those critical questions. That is why the master decided to organize the meeting. They discussed the issues of missing lessons, behavior and academic success. The master was especially strict for Akaki. As for Lekso, she praised the well-brought-up and fair boy and told others that his behavior was just deserving. It was envy that ate Akaki, an aggressive an arrogant boy. The envy resulted in revenge and as the lessons were over the self-conceited teenager decided to stand beside Lekso. He shouldered him again and when Lekso turned his head asked: "Good, good boy, is your nose OK"?! Lekso kept silent. The staidness was so unusual of the age. He had fixed his eyes to Tatia. He followed the girl and came up with her at the end of the street. She noticed him just there and smiled. "Why did not you come to my birthday party"? - asked Tatia. Lekso excused himself and they both kept on walking silently. From time to time the boy looked at her stealthily. They could even hear the hearts of each other beating in the silence. They approached the house where the girl lived. They said goodbye. Their eyes were the ones that could ask questions and give answers then.

Lekso was in the fifth form when Tatia came to their school. A year ago he liked the girl with that pale yellow hair in the corridor. The form master seated her just behind him. Tatia was fond of the boy who always sat with his back turned to the teacher and smiled to her. He was cheerful and witty. The thick, dark hair fell down into his blue eyes. She was a Snow Maiden at the New Year's festive occasion. They told each other about that childlike love that lasted for that last year.

Just in a week the school year would be over. Children had been getting ready for the forthcoming holidays. Akaki approached the boys and girls who had gathered in the campus and with the ironical smile called some of his mates scientists and philosophers. When he reached Lekso he stopped and said: "Hey, Freud, Zigmund, if you are so cool, be as kind as to tell me what I have in my mind about you". Lekso looked at the bully angrily and then turned aside. He did not want to be involved into another conflict, though he realized that it was impossible to avoid a quarrel. He had never seen a man of the type.

-What's up? Leave me alone, guy?! – said Lekso.

-Leave alone?! – Akaki behaved as a boy much elder and continued the gibing:

- You are afraid, right?

Willing to escape from the situation Lekso went to the exit. Akaki crossed his path.

Running? – he said. – Maybe you are a coward.

The last words made Lekso's patience exhausted and he decided that it was the right moment to beat the bore unmercifully and put a finish to the story.

The children from the sixth form had just come out of the room. They all moved towards the exit when Lekso threw his bag away and dashed himself to Akaki with almost lightning speed. He hit the boy right into the face. Lekso was as furious as no one had ever seen him before. Nobody even dared to come nearer. He pushed his rival up and made him fall down again and again. The fight lasted for a few minutes. The sight of their mate who had always been well-wishing affected the children.

The voice of the girl screaming nearby made him take down the fists firmly clenched. He turned to the girl, took her trembling body in his arms and went out with her for Tatia who was so lovely and threatened, so fragile and childish had managed to resign him to go.

The children surrounded them, though no one remembered the unfair troublemaker. They were even glad for most of them had already been disdained and sneered.

In the evening Giorgi called on Lekso. They stood silent and manly on the balcony. Before leaving Giorgi asked Lekso not to go out without him. The boy almost begged to call him in any case. It was somewhat of a hint for Lekso. He nodded and sat down on the stairs of the house. His mother found him sitting there pondering over something.

-Waiting for someone? – He said nothing. Lekso just took Mom's heavy bag and went up the stairs.

The woman was disturbed about the silence and sadness. She tried to get something, though in vain. The boy was silent.

He found no peace that night. In the morning he got up earlier than he usually did. In the yard he saw Tatia and shining with happiness went downstairs. Mom looked out from the balcony and when she saw the girl she had a sigh of relief. It was her who had made her cheerful boy so sad. She saw her son hugging the girl and walking along with her with his arm around her shoulders.

When they entered the campus she said: "Please, Lekso, please"…He knew what she was about. He nodded his agreement and was ready even to beg pardon just to make the fear out of her wonderful eyes. In the corridor they encountered the director. The meeting shook them up and they went up the stairs hurriedly.

At the lessons the children were unusually silent, though no one was aware of what had been going on. The loud, roaring bell by the end of the last lesson made the children jump up their desks. They leapt up as if they were some birds closed in a cage. No one has ever heard such a strange ring in the school. It was not going to stop that symbolic, presage ringing.

Tatia asked Lekso to have a walk in the park situated in the very vicinity of their school. The idea made him glad. Too many children had gathered in the yard. There was Akaki standing among them looking for someone. Lekso and Tatia went past. They had made just ten steps when they felt somebody striding right behind them. She did not have time even to turn, though she noticed somebody standing behind Lekso. She looked up with her eyes made wider with fear and failed to give a cry. A knife pierced into the left part of the boy's back. The sad eyes and the gloomy smile made the girl fall down on her knees.

The noise disturbed everyone in the school. The director and the teachers were running from ne corner of the campus to another. The weeping children tried to keep together as close as possible. On the ground there was Lekso lying on his back. His heart had already stopped beating. Some policemen were dragging Akaki to the police car with his hands fixed together.

The ambulance car carried the body of the sixth former killed by his mate. The sky was bright and the Sun hanging through the devaloka higher than it usually hangs, shared its glints with just ordinary people.

Something had reminded Tatia of the load and long ring that warned them about the untimely death of the boy.

The Crying flowers

She put the magazine aside and looked at the watch. It was 6:40 PM. The television serial was to begin soon and she had to switch the TV on. Right as she made herself comfortable in the chair, somebody knocked at the door. In the doorway there stood a jaded woman carrying a house plant in her hands. The woman looked at her with her poor eyes for a while and then started shyly:

Maybe you want to buy the flower, Madam?! My son has been ill and I need to gather some money for the operation. Please take it!

Diana looked at the wretched woman and got back into the room. She opened a table drawer there, took a stack of money and stuffed it into the stranger's hands. She took the flowerpot. The happy and perplexed woman kissed her palms. "God help you"! -said the hostess snatching her hands from the stranger's ones and turned back.

Behind the closed doors the woman stood on her knees for quite long blessing the hostess whose disinterested help had just made her so happy. It was a huge sum. She was hardly able to drag her legs along, though she had never experienced happiness of the kind. What a merciful person she found that day. When the operation is over and the boy saved she will necessarily come to the woman and thank her. The money is enough to cure her child and that is the only thing she has been seeking for.

Diana put the pot on a windowsill, poured some water to the plant and stroked it. She was really fond of flowers. Her family often went to Manglisi for summer holidays. It was hard to tear oneself away from the nature. She used to go to the meadows, though never dared to pluck the flowers out and took pleasure in looking at their beauty only. Not just because of the affection towards the flowers, but because the stranger needed the money to save her child, Diana gave the woman the sum without a moment's thought. She felt pity for the woman whom misfortune had befallen. She got from an apartment to another to ask people to by the flower for the money that could save her child. As for Diana, her son had been dead for already ten years. No, she had enough money, though all the centers of diagnosis failed to say what the illness was. The boy always trod on his mother's heels. He never stepped aside from his mom. One day when the kid was busy assembling a toy train, Diana ran down the stairs to buy somebread in the basement shop. She did not tell the boy about it beforehand. When she got back she saw that all the folk living in the building had come to her place. Her son had sounded such an alarm that almost everyone had gathered in the flat.

Diana was from a well-to-do family. She was a teacher. She left her job when the boy fell ill. She decided to devote herself to the child. There was nothing left in the world for the woman but the sick kid and the care that he needed so badly.

Her husband used to tell her to take the child to an orphanage and the words often made the woman cry. The boy frequently asked his mom: "Mummy, why are you crying"? Though, she always kept silent. Then he boy changed the question taking an interest in where they were going to take him to. It made Diana's heart bleeding and she started to weep even louder. The broken-hearted woman wept bitterly for there was no one who feeling either pity or love for the diseased child. Even the heart of his own father had hardened for the boy. He was eager to send his son to an orphan asylum. She did her best to make the baby get better, but there was no exact diagnosis for him and therefore it had turned out to be impossible to heal up and save the boy.

When he saw his father, the boy always smiled. The man always met the kid coldly and the unhappy boy had to run to his mom again. The man had met some woman and expressed no interest towards the wife and the child. The adventure was not a secret for their people. It was a fact.

However, all the attempts to save the boy turned out to be just vain. One day the kid unexpectedly died while playing with his toy cars. The woman had an attempt to take her own life, though she was miraculously saved. She spent years in seclusion that finally came to its end that one might consider to be a recovery.

She had already forgotten all about the serial and the whole world around her. She had repotted the flower and was now watering and cherishing it. Touching the beautiful leaves she told the plant about the grief and anxiety that she experienced each day.

A week later nothing had changed. She enjoyed talking with the plant left in her care and did whatever she could to make it glad. In the morning she used to bring the plant in the sunshine and said good night to it as if it had been a son of hers.

Suddenly the flower grew sad. It looked almost lifeless with its leaves all fallen down. Diana lost her heart for she did not make it out what to do with the plant. The cast down woman had no hopes left for the withering flower to be saved.

One morning somebody rang a bell on the door again. In the doorway Diana saw the woman who sold the flower. Though, the guest seemed to be happy for some reason this time. She did not wait for an invitation, just stepped into the apartment and looked into Diana's eyes as if she'd had a piece of good news for her.

You've brought my son back to life. What can I do for you, please tell me?! – asked the happy mom waiting for an answer. "Nothing", - said Diana with a smile glittering her face, - "I'm just happy".

She offered the guest a seat by her side and told her almost everything about her sick boy who died for it was impossible to diagnose the illness. Yes, for Diana she was a very good mother, very, very courageous and brave for she'd saved her child. Diana asked her name. The answer made her start or flinch. There was no doubt about it … she knew someone by the name. But who was it?! When her guest was ready to go, Diana tried to keep her for a minute attempting to gain time to recollect something from the past. She Left her address to the lady, then took off a silver bracelet from her wrist and told the hostess to keep it.

Sitting on her chair Diana all given to reflection looked at the bracelet and tries to recollect something from the old. Hm, Nemsadze Lamara…Lamara…Yes, it was her, the woman her husband used to mention in the context of competition… Lamara and her cheese cakes, Lamara and her French beans, Lamara and her son… It was the child that the two had together. His name was Zviad…the name her husband was always prepared to swear by. And now she had saved the boy. Diana decided to call the woman and ask what the boy's name was.

She hesitated till the evening and finally telephoned her. She heard Lamara's voice through the receiver. The woman was really glad to talk with the benefactress. The question about her son's name made her a bit confused, though the answer made all the things manifest for Diana. It was Levaniko's brother, a boy three years younger than her own child. Yes, it was his brother and it was the woman who had made her cry time and again. However, her husband led a happy life with that other family.

It was May. It was warm. Everything had been flowering. Diana came to the window and looked out through it. She was in a melancholy mood for it was her babe's birthday. She stood there all given up to memories. Suddenly she noticed a tiny pedicle that had come out in the pot. The flower that seemed to have disappeared the whole of yesterday was now alive. Its tiny pale green leaves just radiated happiness.

It was May twenty-five, ten o'clock in the morning when she gave birth to her sonny. She looked down at the watch and tears came out of her eyes running down to the shoot bedewed with that tear-like liquid.

The emergence of the cherished plant was a sign that the soul had missed his mother or had come to thank her for the brother that mom had saved.